WALKING FROM THE SHADOWS

MY JOURNEY WITH POST TRAUMATIC STRESS DISORDER

KEVIN MACOMBER

CONTENTS

The Library of Congress has catalogued editions as follows:

Library of Congress Control Number: 2024927192

Macomber, Kevin A.

Walking From the Shadows: My Journey With Post Traumatic Stress Disorder / Kevin A. Macomber

International Standard Book Numbers:

ISBN 979-8-9922659-0-3 (Paperback)

ISBN 979-8-9922659-2-7 (Kindle eBook)

For information and speaking: wftsinfo@gmail.com

DISCLAIMER

Neither the author, publisher nor any person involved in the preparation of this book are engaged in the rendering of professional advice or services to the individual reader. The concepts, opinions, ideas, information, and suggestions contained in this book are not intended as a substitute for consulting with your physician or other trained, healthcare provider. You are advised to consult with your healthcare providers regarding all matters and aspects of your health. Neither the author, publisher nor any person involved in the preparation of this book shall be liable or responsible for any loss or damage allegedly arising from any information or suggestion in this book. The reader accepts all responsibility if they choose to implement any anecdotal information or process contained herein.

ACCEPTING

THOUGHTS ON ACKNOWLEDGING YOUR STATE OF BEING

As you have chosen to read this book, it is fair to say that you or someone who is close to you has been through some type of trauma. While I am a veteran, this book is by no means focused on veteran-related PTSD. More importantly, while there is a tendency to prioritize the types of trauma, it is from decades of experience that I came to the conclusion to understand that "trauma is trauma." I have seen people go through the most incredible traumatic experiences and have minimal impact, while I have seen other people be completely overwhelmed by minor events. The fact is, for those who have gone through trauma, we all fit somewhere between these two extremes. We are of course unique creatures and craft our own journeys.

The first thing I want to point out is because this was based on many years of journaling, I had a significant amount of information on some topics. You may note that there is a little repetition in the book, but I did this purposefully, because some of the content is so important and can be viewed in different contexts. As well, healing transpires from both redundancy and practice. Depending on the topic or symptom which you may be experiencing, you may need to hear something multiple times for it to register with you. I have done that here and will come at them from different angles. You will also note that I have left room when possible for you to write your THOUGHTS. This book is a tool and encourage you to write in it.

This book is ultimately about accepting one's journey with PTSD, though I use my journey to give reference points to possibly better understand yours. I am neither a counselor nor a PhD, and in fact have no letters behind my last name. I am but a common man who is a veteran and has experienced a great deal of trauma and strife. My journey may or may not be similar to yours and the cause of my trauma is not what this book is about. The purpose of this book is to explain what my journey was like after the trauma, which should share many similarities to those with PTSD. There have been many things that I have heard and experienced regarding my healing, but more importantly, I discuss things I didn't hear and wish I had. This would have expedited my healing process.

I coined this chapter ACCEPTING, as this is really the best place to start. By accepting, I am inferring that you acknowledge something bad happened to you. This event, or events, altered your life and possibly permanently. The impact was so significant that it manipulated how you think, behave, and even live. It permeates the majority of your thoughts throughout the day and it can be so overwhelming, you simply want it to go away. But the reality is the fact that it may never go away and it will oblige you to learn how to manage it for the rest of your life. It may not seem fair, but life is not fair and is often cruel. This is an opportunity for you to not only to get healthier, but to change the narrative of the rest of your life. I chose this survivor mentality and also took the opportunity to make many life-altering changes. Looking back many decades, some of the difficult decisions I made no doubt directed my life to a better position. So let's get going.

This chapter could have also been called COPING, but this is a word that I find vague, because at best, it is an umbrella term like depression, which really does not give an actual state or method to measure or use. While it is commonly used in therapy, support groups and publicly, I feel it says very little about what you actually need to do to move forward. It is freely used in conversations and is more of a general practice or concept that leads one to guess where one is in one's journey and what things one might do to accomplish it. This may be one of the first terms you hear, yet it encompasses many things all of which lend themselves to different approaches, durations, successes, and timing.

I recall early in my healing that someone said to me, "you need to improve your coping skills." I was taken aback at the time and while their intentions were good, I thought to myself, what does that really mean? The reality was, I was doing the very best I could, considering all of the challenges I was facing, as well as the amount and type of counseling I had. More so, my understanding of the concept was far away from where it would be in the future. I was not in denial and was really trying tackle many mental health issues and symptoms. I was cognizant that I couldn't stop the suffering I was experiencing, but from a higher level, I simply wanted the chaotic thoughts and the hemorrhaging, negative feelings to stop. In fact, I really couldn't cope as I didn't fully understand what was going on in order that I could accept the reality of the events that had transpired. And of course, that reality was dismal.

Over many years and thinking about my first exposure to the word coping, the concept seemed peculiar and more so, felt it could infer many things depending on where a person was with their journey. It could make one feel either inadequate or incompetent, or it infers something far more definitive than what it actually is. While that seems somewhat extreme on the surface, the reality is it infers things not being done. Though I would increase my various skills over time, I continued to dislike this word as it really lacked context and seemed to be an oversimplified term developed for psychologists, not patients.

Each person on their journey with PTSD is at a different point of healing. Technically, you can say one needs to improve their coping skills to any person at any point of their healing. And when you use this blanket statement, the novice and the experienced person can interpret this differently, yet for some reason, the support world uses it regularly and flippantly. When broken down to its smaller parts, coping skills includes many methods that cover a very wide array of topics. As there are so many and the diversity of them is so wide, presumably that is why this term is used.

Looking back at how I learned about the healing process, I believe there were a few things that would have helped far more than being told about coping skills. These would have drastically improved and hastened the steps to progress and allowed me to better understand and accept what was going on.

Each person is different, there are many common symptoms and likewise many approaches to each of them. More so, the application of approaches appeared general or even random.

What I could have benefited from was a high-level picture that included a basic understanding of what I could experience in the months and years to come, including those things that were real and perceived. This never happened, and I believe it caused me to "swim" in symptoms for too long as I was trying to grasp something for mental stability. This is not to say a broader conversation about my symptoms never happened, but as you are aware, the healing process from trauma is daunting due to its complexity. It is far more than just symptoms, and the conversations were often generalized as though a list was being followed. It's not that simple, though one thing I attempt to accomplish is to organize the primary things into groups. Breaking up the complexity into smaller manageable pieces, while at the same time showing the interrelationship with each piece, is crucial to making reasonable progress.

At the time I began my counseling, I would have never have expected how long it would take to heal. This was not just a factor of the complexity of my PTSD but the fact that you can only accomplish so much in a 50-minute meeting. If the meetings are spread out, months could be spent on a single topic. This may not be fast enough to adequately stop the anguish and hence much more work will need to be accomplished by yourself. This book goes into that further.

The second thing I needed was the groundwork about how different time periods of your life can continue to impact you. This is particularly important as trauma in different periods of your life may need different approaches. A good analogy of this approach is taking a road trip across a part of the country. Before you go, you look at a map and think about the most practical way to travel. Different highways take you through different topologies and cities, with each having its pros and cons. And like your past, you may have travelled a specific road in the past, yet the road is no longer the same due to development or construction. You may also not even remember the road if it has been some time since you travelled on it. Again, part of your healing is understanding how the events of your life have caused your trauma symptoms to be permanently embedded and even magnified. The events of the past impact the events of the present.

All of this said, what I am speaking of here is the development of a plan (or roadmap) to manage your complex feelings and behaviors. This plan will require you to understand your past experiences, acknowledgement of the details and subsequently to manage them in your present life. This is the approach that I was desiring and simply never had anyone break it down into one broader strategy. And this is why I feel the term coping skills is not a useful one.

Think about all of the obstructions you might experience on a road trip. If there is a major traffic jam in a city, you might take the beltway to circumnavigate it. Possibly on your return trip the traffic will be gone so you can drive through the city. This imagery should help you understand that you do not necessarily use the same tactics to handle the same symptoms that occur in different parts of your life. Fundamentally, the structure and content of this book does that, and while each chapter is independent, you may find some chapters lend themselves to a sequence. You will note that I capitalize a chapter's name so you can delve further into a concept.

Possibly the best chapter to start with is UNDERSTANDING. Before you can move into a period of recovery, you are going to need to get a realistic understanding of your trauma. In my case, I went through a great deal of trauma and it impacted multiple areas of my life over a good amount of time. I was in fact dealing with layers of PTSD. It was quite complex, and its symptoms were absolutely overwhelming. I like to use the phrase "swimming in symptoms." No matter where you are in your understanding, I would work to break it down into time periods. This may not be a perfect method, but it will allow you to wrap your arms around smaller portions. In my case, I had trauma in my childhood, during my military service and post-military. The causes were quite different from one another, and while they shared some of the same impacts, there were unique ones, as well.

With regard to symptoms, you may have a number of them. If you are like me, your symptoms may be quite fluid. Meaning, one day Symptom A was elevated and the others were difficult but holding level. A week later Symptom A was holding level and one or more of the others had increased. This, of course, can be exhausting and confusing. It can also drive your anxiety and other negative feelings. And while you may not see value in doing it intently, the practice of journaling is crucial and will help you and your counselor in the future. You can do this as vague or as detailed as you want, but this can help you to understand your current mental state and more importantly, to help you identify patterns. There may be certain times of the day, triggers, people, etc. that make you feel uncomfortable. As my layers of PTSD covered a couple decades, the various layers were inherently difficult to understand. Writing put a good deal of clarity to my PTSD. It also simply got it out of my head.

Understanding is coupled with acceptance. My life was a complete mess when I broke down. I literally was at a loss what to do. Possibly this is where you are, too. I could not see any end to my situation, and that no doubt magnified the intensity of the despair. What I can say from experience is that no matter your knowledge and personal experiences, you are going to need help from sources beyond yourself. In the chapter HELPING, I cover my approaches to finding help. In the current world, there still is some stigma to mental health issues, but it is a fraction of what it used to be. I'm not trying to discount that it may require some discretion and extra effort on your part, but there is a much broader acceptance publicly of the topic, and the resources are extensive. What resource you use will be dictated by the type and severity of your trauma(s), but the key thing that must happen is addressing it quickly. The availability of some resources is limited, such as getting a psychologist appointment quickly, but there are other resources, some of which are free, that can be used in parallel. This strategy may be one of the most important as it is very much like a road trip. You will not only need to understand where you are headed to but acknowledge the obstacles you might face.

During this early period, you may need to make some difficult decisions to safeguard yourself from more anxiety or traumatizing events. I discuss this in the chapter CUTTING, where I provide an overview of the many things I chose to remove from my life. In my case this included people, and this did not happen quickly. Removing things, activities, people, etc. from your life can be quite difficult, particularly if it is family. I probably would have cut off some people quicker than I did, but I also did not have complete information either. I didn't have a deep enough understanding of what was happening psychologically to me and the subsequent impact, nor did I have a friend or counselor who could help me decipher what was going on fast enough. Again, there is much more information and guidance online today, where one can simply enter the topic into a search engine and immediately be fed thoughts and ideas on the matter. As an example, some things triggering me were obvious, but other things like gaslighting were not. The latter took some time to figure out. Once those details came together, I quickly acted upon it.

That said, this is where having an understanding by time period really does help. You will have different strategies and tactics to address those triggering you from the past and present. For example, if a person from your past caused your trauma, you should contemplate stopping your interactions with them moving forward. Sometimes this becomes very complicated if it is a spouse with kids or possibly a family member. If there is a person in the present who is triggering you based on what happened in your past, you have a number of options as to how to manage it. This could include having a conversation, establishing boundaries, or going as far as ending the relationship. I have done all of these, though in my later years this became quite infrequent as I had done a fairly good job qualifying those I let into my life.

One thing you will need to learn to manage is your behavior. If your trauma influenced your life enough, it will more than likely influence you to have some negative behaviors. And while your trauma may have hurt you significantly, you are still responsible for how you act. Some people may act violently towards others or themselves, or it may simply be an elevated level of aggressiveness or assertiveness. There may be a willingness to verbally attack others, and this is probably the most common. This sometimes includes innocent people whom we are letting loose on. And the list of things you probably should not do is extensive, and if you are honest with yourself, you already know what your tendencies are.

Understandably, you may be quite angry and frustrated. And it goes without saying that you will need to really guard your behavior and comments publicly, to include social media. This not only includes friends, family and acquaintances, but particularly the people you work with. Your job is your lifeline to keeping yourself financially afloat, and whether you believe so or not, your negative behavior may be projecting even subtly. Very early in my troubles, the absolutely best advice came from two people. The first was "less is more." The premise of this is to keep your behavior and actions to the minimal level possible in the public environment. It also means to be very self-aware to ensure you are not acting out, even subtly. In my case, I thought I did do this, but I don't think I did it well as I should have. I wish at the time I had a confidant sit down with me and mentor me. So I am going to do it here by saying to become quite mindful of how you are acting.

To this, the second piece of advice was to be kind. I did not see the incredible power of this at the time. While you really do have the right to be angry, controlling what you say, or in this case what you don't say, is going to help you significantly. Admittedly, I didn't always hold my tongue and it was of course filled with some degree of retaliation. Some of this was due to immaturity, but some was due to lack of control. This wasn't extreme, but it was probably based on the premise that I wanted the person to hear, and possibly acknowledge how I was hurt. But it was the wisdom of one person who really changed my thinking of this approach. If you don't lash out at someone, despite whether you think it is valid or not, you are not put in a position of later regretting something you said, or even worse, have it used against you in the future. I cannot count the number of times I have done this and most certainly over many years, I can see in hindsight that it permitted me to have a clearer conscience.

Another area of your life you need to manage is self-care. For myself, I failed to take care of myself during my breakdown. If you don't care for yourself, it is going to magnify your symptoms and reactions. And from knowing many people with PTSD, most experience some of this. As I discuss in the chapter RESTING, sleep and any form of rest evaded me for years. This absolutely slowed my thinking processes as I was fatigued all the time. It also left me irritable, though years into it, I had learned to suppress my reactions. My depression was also extensive, and at the time it reduced my desire and ability to do some of the most basic things, such as eating or physical activity, like walking. I still recall how absolutely daunting it was to function. At the time, I don't even know if I understood the consequences, but the depression had clouded much of my logical thinking anyhow. I discuss this in the chapters FALLING and WALKING.

One sensitive topic that falls into self-care is self-medicating. During my military years I was drinking a great deal, and typically binge drinking on weekends or when I was on a short break during deployment. In hindsight, I was drinking a tremendous amount and while I never became an alcoholic, I most certainly had a drinking problem that could have led me to this condition. After my military period, my life was evolving and I recognized that drinking was not good for me. By the time I was in college, the circumstances of being very busy with studies and work and as well, not having much disposable income helped this situationally.

It was a short while after I was married that I met an elderly man who gave me some wisdom on this issue. He asked "are you better off with it or without it?" In my situation, it was absolutely clear that I was better off without it. This decision was out of practicality. As I was dealing with so many symptoms and the reality of a busy life with kids, I couldn't afford to lose any more mental capacity, particularly what I had worked hard to stabilize. More so, being on medications that don't work well with it could potentially harm me. Over time, I just lost interest in it. The reason I am bringing this up early in the book is if you have a substance abuse issue, you are going to need to come to terms with it so you can address your other PTSD symptoms. And I'm here to tell you don't be ashamed, because it is quite common. If you choose to use AA or NA, you actually may find some of the best support available.

The last item you will need to accept is that your memories are not going to go away. What will change however, is how you manage them. I vividly recall feeling burdened to the point that I never thought I would escape the torment. However, over time this did improve. I discuss this in the chapters FALLING and FORGETTING. While you possibly can't foresee it now, you most likely will have an opportunity to take your tragedies and use them to do good in the future. You have more buried strength that will create a new person as well as a more positive future.

THOUGHTS:

CUTTING

THOUGHTS ON REMOVING TRIGGERS

Most of the details during the weeks following my breakdown are a blur and I wrote very few comments. I honestly wish I had written more about it as it would have been helpful to not only stitch together my state of mind, but things I may have done to survive.

However, there are a few things I did, whether purposefully, functionally or coincidentally, that probably helped manage some of the hemorrhaging chaos. Though unfortunately, it would get worse as time progressed. And though I may be a bit repetitive on this, it is extremely difficult to put words to the complexity of what I was going through. At the time, I was going through several big life changes, which at this point, I still have no other reference point or experiences to compare it too. By life changes, I mean changes in relationships, family, moving, work, etc., all of which cause a great amount of stress and anxiety. I do however know at the time I had not yet given up and had to be frantically grasping at things that would have brought me stability. I can say this as I had not yet done anything inappropriately drastic, as in attempting suicide, and more so, was still going to work and functioning, albeit at a low level.

I would not fully appreciate the impact of what I learned until several years later when I was underway with my recovery to wholeness and the healing work on my severe PTSD. And admittedly, what I am going to share may rest uneasy with you, but I ask that you at least think through these thoughts. They are of course my thoughts, but having embraced them for nearly three decades, I can say they definitively helped me and I credit it as one of the most important parts of my recovery process. That is being able to cut belongings, places and people, which may include a family member, spouse, long-time friend, colleague, or acquaintance. I chose the word "cutting" for this chapter in lieu of "removing," because this was such a difficult thing to do. These actions really hurt me both mentally and emotionally, but deep down I understood the necessity to do it.

The thoughts I give here may on the surface seem to conflict with one's faith or social mores, I disagree and will walk you through my rationalization. It is obvious that one may not want to remove things from their life, particularly when they were created in a positive manner, or at least you thought they were. But what transpired is that I really had little choice as I was in a survival mode and needed mental relief. It was very difficult separating the past memories, as I was unable to discern what was real and what wasn't. In my case, and again looking back upon it decades later, the faster you can eliminate or reduce things that trigger your past, the better. Specifically, the short phrase "cut early, cut deep" is the approach I took, but admittedly these took years implement as more detail revealed itself.

The easiest thing to cut are belongings. At the time when my breakdown was deepening, most of my belongings took me back to past memories, many of which I was confused whether they were real or not. I remember starting in the bathroom, which had the least attachment, and literally taking drawers and throwing most of the contents into the dumpster. As the weeks progressed, I went from room to room going through items and boxes. Almost all of it brought back memories and magnified my suffering. Every last picture, memento or item, no matter the size, that had a nuance of the past was tossed. And the hardest by far were the pictures as they were a snapshot of the past. I still recall holding them in my hand and dropping them in the trash one by one. I was in complete disbelief. By the time I was done it was time to move. The vast amount of stuff that once took a moving truck to move, took but a couple car loads.

The second thing I cut were places I connected to the past. This in part was due to the fact I had moved so far away and the distance really precluded me going by places that triggered my memories. Years later I visited a couple places, mostly through work, but my emotional attachment had long been severed. But this is not the case for everyone, as there are a variety of places from geographic locations and events that can trigger you. If this is the case, simply stay away and keep your mind on the fact that you will be creating new memories that will overshadow the old.

For me, and probably for most, the aspect of removing people from our lives is the hardest, but this is the most important. Objects and places don't trigger you as much as you letting them do that to you. You have control over that. People are different, as they can overtly cause you more trauma or at a minimum, magnify your pain. Kahlil Gibran said, "if you love somebody, let them go." But, I would argue that this is incomplete and would add "if you love yourself, let them go." If you are to heal, you may very well need to make some extremely difficult decisions, but your future life and mental health may depend on you doing so.

There would eventually be a number of people I removed from my life to lessen the chance of being drawn back into parts of my past and furthermore, triggering bad or false memories. Some were done with different intentions, meaning my selection was done knowing how they had negatively impacted me and a couple others were done more casually as I didn't have the bandwidth to deal with them. And so began the process of removing people from my life, or in other ways did not let them into my current life, who were not positively contributing to my wellbeing. Some of these decisions were very difficult while others were far more pragmatic. And this wasn't solely based on who they were to me, but what they represented.

And while the focus may be on removing people from your life, what you are in fact doing is removing yourself from your past life. If you want to move forward, you may be obliged to remove some people from your past. This really may not be optional, and having known and observed those who did not do this, they didn't appear to fully heal and were left in a state of having to accommodate or deal with an array of chaos. One of the best analogies I can give is the story of Lot's wife who turned around, looked at her past, and turned into a pillar of salt. If you do not change who is influencing your life, it will be very hard to move forward, if not impossible. You will essentially be frozen in time. In fact, I would use this story and say to myself: "will this person turn me into a pillar of salt?" Another question you could ask is "how will this person turn me into a pillar of salt?" I think this speaks for itself.

The hardest thing I had to remove, and by far, was family, because it would involve a number of people, some of whom were malevolent. It is said that you can pick your friends, but you can't pick your family. I disagree with this. As I cover in the chapters TRUSTING and UNDERSTANDING, my family situation was quite poor and had been for a long time. But the level of dysfunction within my extended family was also complex, and while I surmised many things, it would take many years to uncover the full details. I would cut my ties with my father, my mother, my grandmother, an uncle, and a couple of in-laws. And yes, on the surface this seems almost imaginable, but for a variety of reasons was well justified, and to this day I have almost no regrets. But for the purpose of cutting family, I will speak solely of my parents.

By any standard, it is hard to comprehend a child cutting off a parent from their life. Besides giving me life, my father failed me on so many levels and the damage he caused was significant. Could there have been reparations? Absolutely, I believe it could have been possible. Yet he was neither emotionally capable nor wanting. This was also compounded by the fact that by the time I remarried, I had worked diligently on myself and had made progress on creating a new person. After several years, I was barely the person who I had been and had embraced much of the fundamentals of what this book is about. As time further progressed, the divide became wider and wider. Then my father passed away. I remember the day he died feeling a great sense of relief.

My mother was far more difficult to cut, but our relationship was futile. For years, I pitied my mother and encouraged her to leave my father. But she was enabled and unwilling. And even though I wanted a relationship with her, and to salvage a life for her, it wasn't meant to be. If I wanted to visit her, I was obliged to be with my father. If she were to visit me alone, there would be retribution for her if he didn't come along. The situation was further complicated as she began showing signs of dementia at a young age, which set in quickly. And while she had a tendency to confabulate for a number of years, her condition set in and would continually deteriorate. So it was time and distance that created a divide. By the time my father passed, she was incoherent and did not know who I was. Within a few years, her dementia progressed to Alzheimer's and she passed away.

In hindsight, cutting other family members, namely my mother's family proved prudent. This, however, proved hard, because I did have some positive memories with them, more than with my own parents. But as wisdom and worldliness kicks in, your ability to interpret details and situational things significantly increases. For me, there became a pool of details, that once connected and namely repeated, it gave me much clarity and concern. The first, and most difficult to accept, was the fact my mother's extended family was quite aware of what was going on with my childhood, and more so, they did nothing. Specifically, one noted in a casual conversation that they were discussing how they should get involved to assist my mother and my one uncle said there was a conversation "do you want them?" He was specifically saying that about my mother, sister and I and that we would either be a burden or impact their lifestyle. Hearing this and many other things, made cutting them off easier.

The second thing that was harder to accept, was learning what was really going on during those difficult years. Specifically, the positive memories I had may have not been real. As in they were behaving or faking their actions to keep the chaos and true feelings at bay. My gut instinct and approaches proved correct. All of this was a coordinated strategy referred to as "family scapegoating." My mother's family loathed my father, but this rippled over to me. I can reflect back to illogical events as a child, and as the details increased, could see the malevolence that was transpiring.

Again, this came from gathering information by asking very pointed and quite honestly, very difficult and sensitive questions. It was however, listening carefully, noting the word choices used and subsequently tying the pieces together. This of course is not easy to do and it may make you feel vulnerable at the time. But, I can't emphasize enough how important it is to understand who is on your side and being supportive of you. In my case, I asked very specific questions about events and people, and the way and manner they answered them, clearly indicated they were trying evade or deflect them. I ultimately ended up cutting off all of my mother's family, with the last one being many years out. The little family I thought I had, were not really family at all.

I also had to deal with the memories from my first marriage that failed. Over many years now, I have met scores of divorced people whose PTSD has been impacted by this in varying levels. Some of the divorces were amicable, but many ended poorly, with many of the relationships being abusive. Some were incredibly sad, while others provided a great sense of relief. Having observed others who successfully moved forward from difficult marriages, no matter how you may quantify that, many of them embraced a strategy of permanently ending the relationship. And for those who came from a bad situation and had children, varying strategies were employed, with distance and rules being the primary ones. In my case, this was simply a very sad time for me and required some time to move forward from both good and bad memories. But this mirrored so many aspects of my life memories, which were hard to discern whether they were real or not. I would eventually just accept it as a failure. As there is so much material written divorce, the key thing I want to emphasize is the degree it can impact your PTSD and for some period of time.

The next group of people I removed from my life were friends and acquaintances. Some of this was not necessarily due to how they acted, but the natural part of life where you get busy, move away or life just moves onward. This may simply be losing interest in pursuing the relationship. There were, however, people that I simply grew away from. People who I once was close too, became less attached as their beliefs and actions were incompatible with an evolution to healing. And this is as crucial, if not more so, than your family due to the frequency of interactions, as they are your support network. Are they helping you heal and grow, or are they pulling you backwards? This is hard to do, particularly if you have positive memories. In my case, my moral compass and values had tightened. I couldn't profess being the person I wanted to be or strive to be, while continuing to engage with people who weren't generally heading in that direction. The more tacit issues are easier. If you are struggling with an addiction, say alcoholism, you can't continue hanging out with people who drink a great deal. It may even be hard to be with people who drink a little as this can trigger memories of the past. If you are struggling with PTSD or depression, you must be with people who will help you grow from your symptoms and negative behaviors.

One interesting metric that aided me in developing my circle of friends has been social media. And there are good and bad experiences there. One thing that has shocked me is how some people, whom I have known for a long time, actually act when under duress and are unable to control their emotions and subsequently the things they say. For example, I knew a man for about 10 years in a hobby that I partake in. One day I saw a post that left me speechless. And I think we all know people who grow a few inches behind their computer screen with the things they say, but his comments were far past the point of acceptability. What I saw in this case was unspeakable in terms of its ugliness and nastiness. I immediately unfriended them.

Now you may be thinking by all of these strict rules, how can you have any friends. That is not the case and it requires some work to find them. The first place is finding an organization or group that shares common issues. If you have an addiction, going to AA or NA, can provide the closest and quickest group of people who understand you. Though I never had a substance addiction, I have been to many AA meetings and can tell you I have met many genuine people battling their demons. My level of respect for these people was and remains high. If you are struggling with PTSD, finding a support group is imperative. I have made a few close friends who I not only understood intimately, but they understood me. I go into this extensively in the chapter HELPING.

The second place that comes to mind for most is a Church, but remember, that is where broken people can go to, and that is not perfect. What I would say is to focus on an organization that is productive. Meaning, the group is doing positive things for themselves as a whole or the community. This may be a Church, but suggest evaluating one with missions or outreach programs. Service work brings like-minded people together, though as you are aware, you still have to be careful of group politics, so a long-standing group might be the most stable environment. It may also give you a group of people who are not necessarily struggling with the same issues like you are. And I think it is important to find average people going through life and facing the normal aspects of life. They will not be perfect, but you can learn skills and behaviors from those who have not gone through trauma.

Now to be quite clear, cutting people from your life is not easy and may be quite difficult. Of course, if it is easy, and you don't get much pushback or ugliness, then you know your decision was right. But the one thing I want to mentally prepare you for is retaliation. While friends are probably going to be easier than family, there still can be some degree of overt actions towards you in the form of verbal manipulation, lies or just ugly words. In the case of an uncle, he turned outright ugly and became both manipulative and overtly trying to cause trouble for me in the family. The details are not important, but with him, he was outright lying and conspiring with others in the family. As noted above, this is referred to as family scapegoating, but my gut instinct told me what was going on, though it took many years to see what he had been doing. And of course, it was still hard to see someone I had once cared for and who I thought had cared for me, act in such a way. It was very difficult to process. But as time progressed, my interactions with him all but faded to none and two decades later, I will tell you my decision to cut him off was very prudent. I would subsequently learn that is how he had acted much of his life. His behavior was his to own and if I am grateful for one thing, I never retaliated, though it did come to mind. I wanted to tell him off and call him out, but I realized the act of doing that would show I cared about the relationship. I didn't care, but more so couldn't care.

Another area that is hard to cut are the actual memories. I have a number of bad memories of these people, but I did have positive memories, though as noted, they were staged. Actually, I have a lot of bad memories, some which have caused much damage and still linger lightly. And you will not be able to remove the bad memories, but you can compartmentalize them, put them to the side, acknowledge them, but leave them there. This will take practice to the point of saying, "I'm done with this and am not going to let it live rent free in my head anymore." But it will also require you to create new and positive memories. This is not as simple turning the bad memories off and the good ones on, but slowing the bad and picking up the pace of good ones. Hence, why being surround by a "positive" group of people is so important.

One topic I have been asked is how to remove people from your life. The first group are the easiest and those are the ones that overtly do things that are outright wrong. Of course, you should try to see if the relationship can be fixed by communicating your feelings, setting boundaries, or even going to counseling. A person's willingness to mend a broken relationship is a good sign and possibly shows their ability to correct themselves or, from a more humble perspective, admit their shortcomings. In my case, none of the people I was dealing with showed any remorse. Specifically, they viewed the current situation was solely my fault and due to my actions. Of course, I was partly to blame as that is part of normal human interactions. But the fact they took no responsibility further showed the depth of their behavior. The degree of narcissism I was facing was significant and this is a topic you should learn about so you can protect yourself.

The second group of people are those that act out periodically. You may not be sure how to deal with them or respond to their actions. Moreso you may struggle to understand what their behaviors mean. In this case, I suggest slowing the relationship down, namely by reducing the frequency of interactions. In doing this, this gives you more time to think through about your decision, but more importantly, it will let you assess how they react. It might come down to the fact they don't do anything, possibly inferring they don't care much about the relationship, or conversely, they could start acting out. And that is what you want to uncover. If their negative behaviors start increasing, then this will help make your decision.

Removing people out of your life is very difficult, but your well being and improvement of your mental health will require it. Make sure to journal and take notes of the occurrences. Remember, it is your mental health verses theirs. If you stay with negative or manipulative people, they will slow or stall your path to wholeness, and even worse, they may take you back to a place you have tried so hard to get away from.

THOUGHTS:

DRIFTING

THOUGHTS ON DISSOCIATION AND COGNITIVE LOSSES

By my early fifties I travelled a great deal for work, often 80-100 nights per year. This was in addition to daily travel to clients. It would be common to arrive home late on Thursday or Friday evening, only to head back out on Sunday or Monday. The grind of the travel on top of the workload began to cause me fatigue to the point that I never felt rested. There were times it took all the powers in the world to get me out of bed on the weekend, even though I knew that I still had family responsibilities that had to be done.

But something was changing, and my mind started becoming less able to focus. At first, I simply attributed this to being burned-out from work, which in part it was, but this was different. There was a sporadic fuzziness that started increasing during the day that would ebb and flow, but then it would include instances where my mind just momentarily disappeared.

While those with PTSD might want to hear if you do certain things it will get better, the reality is that it may not and that is what was happening to me. While the cause and timing of my decline was never really fully documented or diagnosed, and I use that word for lack of any other, my feeling is it was the same factors that caused my breakdown. Those being stress, duress and fatigue coupled with my depression.

The best example I can give is that during my breakdown, it was like a tire blowing out and disabling your car. You can't fix the tire, but you I can put a spare on to get you to the repair shop to fix or buy a new one. The difference at this point in my life is that the good parts of my life were like a tire with a slow leak. I knew the tire could lose air, but I did maintenance on it to get a few more miles out of it. In fact, I was doing well, considering the evolving diagnosis of my mental health. I had a fairly stable family life, held a good job and had some interests in my spare time that I enjoyed. But the stress and fatigue were taking a toll, and I felt my cognition slipping even though I couldn't fully express the changes I was feeling.

In the chapter LEARNING, I discuss some of the difficulties I had finding a therapist that I could connect to, but more so, one that would take a more proactive interest in digging deep and trying to understand what was causing these feelings. It was my pursuit of a new and younger therapist that would eventually begin to give clarity to what may be going on.

What I came to understand, and honestly I'm not sure why I didn't pick up on this much earlier as it is somewhat obvious, but is that different conditions can share the same symptoms. So if you are working on an issue like anxiety, it can be caused by neurological and medical issues, and likewise can be enhanced by depression. My drifting was similar and was being impacted by traumatic brain injury (TBI), neuro-psychological issues as well as my PTSD.

I am not going to pretend to be expert on these topics, so I am not going to go into depth on them as I will most certainly do an injustice to them, but what I am an expert on is my personal experience dealing with them. And as I have mentioned before, it is important to develop a basic understanding of how these symptoms or issues may have happened and what you can reasonably do to manage them.

The first issue impacting me is TBI. I am starting with this not because it is the most prevalent, but it is probably the easier one to identify qualifying events. Many veterans, first responders and those in accidents sustain head injuries, but it is the significant ones that possibly make the diagnosis quicker. In my case I've had multiple qualifying events. During the service I was involved in one accident and also hit my head multiple other times doing my job. I don't remember my reactions so well, but at the time I was in excellent physical condition, and like someone who plays a sport and gets hit, you just get up and keep going. During the accident, it probably would have been good to have been checked out, but there really wasn't a method and from the outside I looked fine. So I kept going.

Later in life, my depression had me in a dark place and fell into my second breakdown. It was at this point that self-harm began, which generally involved me purposefully hitting my head. While this of course is not the way to deal with depression, the reality is the flashbacks and night terrors were at their peak. I couldn't stop them and because of my inability to sleep, I was literally being torn apart. I wanted the images to stop and they wouldn't subside, so I hit my head trying to knock them out. I am open about this as self-harm and suicidal ideation can be part of both depression and PTSD. This was the actual point I began with the Veterans Administration (VA) in an effort to not only get help, but also to seek information as to what was going on and subsequently to figure out how I could gain some control for managing them.

By my forties, subtle behaviors emerged, though at the time I was not connecting them fully to my past. The strangest action was my balance, which by the way, still continues. When either standing still or walking, I would simply lose my balance and fall over. Another, which was more gradual, was the loss of smell. As I progressed through my forties, other signs like delayed speech and sensitivity to light began impeding me. This of course was on top of other symptoms like fatigue, anxiety and tinnitus (ringing of the ears), which were already embedded, but are also symptoms of TBI and other mental health issues.

By the time I was in my early fifties, the symptoms were quite magnified, but the one advantage I had was that through therapy, I had developed varied skills to better manage them. The symptoms that really began to increase were short term memory and concentration losses that were to the point they were mimicking dementia. I would be tested for dementia, but those tests came up negative. When I was fully clear, I was fully alert and sharp, but that was becoming less often. At work, I was still at peak performance and my thoughts, often focused on highly complex designs and projects, was slipping. Part of this was poor sleep and exhaustion and part was simply being burned out from my job. I didn't like the company I was working for, but due to a number of life factors I had to stay with it. And so it was during this time a symptom , which is still present, really took a foothold and remains present, . And that is my mind drifting.

At first, I thought this drifting was dissociation. I have come to understand that in part it was. I was feeling disconnected from myself. I struggled, feeling pain at times, and I suffered a fairly broad amnesia, which also continues to this day. It had me forgetting many things about myself and time periods of my past. Some of those things weren't that old either. But this was different from what I could learn about dissociation. I was experiencing symptoms that came and went in slow, nonrhythmic waves at all times of the day. And to use another car analogy, think about driving a car that needs a wheel alignment. As you drive down the road and depending on the road's condition, the car veers towards or across the painted road lines. In response you make slight pulls on the steering wheel to pull yourself back into your lane. There is a term "brain fog" which could be applied to this, but it was the random turning on and off that didn't seem to fit this term. And that is how I coined this term "drifting," because I began randomly experiencing this all day long.

When I look back at this change it was quite significant, as it was impacting every aspect of my day. But then another two patterns arose. The first was where I was disappearing from my thoughts. Meaning, that no matter what I was doing, my mind would literally turn off for a second or two. And I literally mean every situation. The strangest, which is still prevalent, is that I can stop talking mid-sentence for a second or two and then start back up where I stopped. My family and close friends were extremely helpful, as they knew intimately of my PTSD and gently helped me out of it when it occurred. And for those who didn't know me, this projected as a quirky behavior. As I was aware of it and it was manageable, if they were the right person, I would let them know what was going on. This however, increased in frequency and became a permanent behavior that I have come to live with. The second issue is that my tinnitus became more severe, and by severe, I mean it was so loud that it was overwhelming my cognition. At times, which also continues to this day, it is so loud that it drowns out all other sounds. None of this, particularly in its totality, fits well with a job that requires significant thought processes. Ultimately, this began the downfall of my career, and it unraveled quickly.

What is complicated here is trying to understand what the root cause is and what can be done. As noted before, many of these behaviors can be attributed to TBI, neuro-psychological issues or PTSD. As my situation was so complicated, and because it is so difficult to make one succinct assessment, it evolved to being a combination of all three. If you are experiencing what I refer to as 'head issues,' it is unlike other illnesses as the doctor is limited to how they can observe your behaviors and what they can accomplish with medical assessments like scans. The behaviors are also problematic, because they may not happen to the same intensity or frequency when you are with the doctor. Hence, there have been times when an assessment was done and despite the symptoms, the results came up inconclusive.

My journey to understand this was difficult at best and despite seeking therapy, I did not feel I was becoming any clearer as to what was going on. My frustration with these behaviors increased, but what was really peaking my frustration was how so many professionals, both psychologists and psychiatrists, weren't giving much clarity to this either. To give balance to this criticism, I was responsible for articulating what I thought was going on, and in hindsight, I believe I did a fairly good job of this. Considering I was a patient and not a trained professional, my understanding and limited experiences as to what was going on in my head was leaning in the right direction. Trying to explain even what a headache feels like is not easy. In meeting with therapists in recent years, I ask the question, "is what I'm saying clear?"

In the chapter LEARNING, I discuss that much of my knowledge came from my own researching. This approach, which I strongly recommend, is what expanded both my understanding and vocabulary. What I write in this chapter, mostly came from this approach. and only limited parts came from therapists. While you might think you deserve more from your providers, if you are within the VA system, you need to temper that expectation significantly. The VA is a behemoth, medical system and you are but a number. This could possibly be said of other large medical organizations as well. Your expectations will be set by your knowledge and actions, and at no time should you believe that they will be proactive and do any more than what your specific session or appointment is set to do. Think of this as a modified triage, where they get you in, assess you and move you along.

When it comes to head issues, my experience with the VA has

been average at best. While I have had some excellent psychiatrists and therapists, I have had far more that were not sufficient to my needs. When I began my own research, what really stood out was what they weren't saying versus what they were. Specifically, it was my questions about my symptoms that were leading the conversations. I came to appointments prepared with terms, questions and notes on all. I have little doubt they were taken aback and particularly, by the depth and clarity of my comments and the questioning of their comments. In hindsight, it is fair to say that my efforts were moving my treatment along more than their involvement. I personally had issues where providers were not reading my previous notes, but to be fair, it also appeared at times the system they put the notes into, was not easy to navigate. My advice is to specifically ask the provider that you are meeting with whether they read your historical notes. I've caught a couple not doing this, and it means they weren't prepared to meet with me. Of course, you will feel slighted that you are not getting a truly comprehensive assessment.

I discuss in the chapter HELPING, that your ability to grow is in part dependent on your efforts to understand what is technically going on with you. Meaning, you shouldn't expect to go to a counselor or doctor and expect them to impart all of the information. This is where I think you hear about patients not connecting with their provider. Our assessments can be quite complex and their input is only as good as what we tell them or they can draw out of us. My path forward to diagnosis and treatment could have been situational, but feel a good portion of it was due to me reading and researching a significant amount of material. Having both engineering and project management skills, I have been trained to understand complex issues and ask respective pertinent questions to remediate them. This is actually a fairly strong skill I possess, but of course many people don't have them. No matter your skills, you are going to have to learn to advocate for yourself and become comfortable doing this. Think about your communication skills and how you can leverage or improve them.

As my symptoms evolved, the VA relinquished part of the treatment plan to an outsourced medical provider. As I had before, I prepared by gathering all the materials of the past, so I could help the new doctor help me. I knew for a fact that while they should have access to most of the materials, they might not find them. Moreso, as my assessments moved outside the VA, there was at times a breakdown of communication between the two providers. In two instances, I literally had to handhold the test from the third-party and call my VA doctor to tell them it was ready for them to review. Another time, my doctor could not find the test and I was obliged to call the VA's Patient Records and tell them to retrieve it from the third-party and give it to my doctor. I cannot say how prevalent this is, but events like this will anger and demoralize you. At a minimum, they will test your patience. You cannot take this personally and you have to assume things like this require your involvement.

If you have head issues and if there is a third-party involved, this is my advice. First, do not expect the "system" to work efficiently. Look at your assessment or treatment as a triangular relationship with the VA, the third-party provider and yourself on each point. When it comes to your responsibility, there are several things you need to do. The first is to document all of your actions and appointments in a notebook. For each item, you should annotate the meeting, the time, who was present and all contact information. You will then annotate key items and then itemize any actions required by yourself and the provider. Before you end the meeting, go back through those and get them to confirm each one. This action will prove extremely valuable, because you simply cannot keep all of this information in your head. It also lets you hold the provider accountable. The contact information is also important, because in recent years, I have personally experienced a reduced response rate with phone calls and emails. You may be obliged to chase them. All of this together, will have you becoming a project manager for yourself.

The next thing you want to do is gather documentation. The notes your provider puts in their system are your notes, and you are entitled to them. While the doctor or nurse may not be able to easily do this, VA Patient Records can. This documentation should also include any scans. By having these documents, you can see how accurate or articulate they are, but also if the provider is understanding your situation as you think they are. Possibly you said something that was not clear or they simply interpreted it differently. But as noted before, if you go outside the system, you have notes to give to that provider, and this may help them expedite your assessment. Most outside providers are aware of the quirkiness of communication with the VA and will most likely be grateful for your assistance. Regarding the scans, from a medical perspective they are important, because depending on their timing and frequency, they can give a base line to new scans indicating whether or not there have been changes.

The last task is to have an advocate, which could be a family member or close friend. There came a period of time where my care at the VA was both inadequate and unacceptable. At one point, my son called both the VA's patient advocacy. My son was aware of my treatment issues and due to his concern, called patient advocacy on my behalf, and this had some positive effects. While I do not like the "squeaky wheel" approach, at times it is necessary in the VA system or other large bureaucratic entities. With the limited resources available, sometimes you simply have to speak up to be heard. If you have a real issue, be thoroughly prepared with details. This is where the notebook becomes invaluable. But remember, patient advocacy is not your therapist, so manage your emotions accordingly.

The other use of an advocate is to bring them to the meeting or appointment when appropriate. If you aren't aware, you are not permitted to record a session, but you are allowed to bring a person who essentially becomes a witness. As I was questioning my care, I asked my wife to come to the meeting and listen to what was going on and to help me understand if what I was being told was adequate. One inherent benefit of this approach is that your advocate may also be able to help contribute to your content. Meaning, if you have a strong fight or flight response, you may not be able to clearly remember or articulate adequate information to your provider while being heavily questioned. But in my case, my wife confirmed my concerns, not because she was my wife, but because the content of what was being discussed was actually inadequate. Coupled with your notes, you will have the leverage to hold the VA or other provider to some level of accountability and responsivity.

From having very complex issues and having been through so many providers, my advice for care is to work as hard as possible to get care for your head issues outside of the VA. While I have noted much criticism of the VA, I also understand that in context that one can only expect so much from them. When I have gone outside the VA, the caliber of care is notably different, and as you move into neuro-psychological topics, my personal observation is that they are significantly better. In my case, it appeared the VA did not have the skills or personnel, which obliged me to go outside the VA system. This ultimately worked to my advantage.

My head issues eventually became severe enough that the VA rated me "unemployable." This rating did not rest easy with me as I had been working since I was a kid. During my professional years, work also defined a significant portion of my identity. Understandably, this gave me a sense of pride as a number of things that I accomplished were substantial. I was sharp, innovative and successful. Being told that you are really no longer those things is not easy to hear and can make you question your self-value.

The one thing that helped this transition away from work was that I no longer liked my job and in lieu of finding a new one, it became time to find a new purpose. Living with and managing this situation required many approaches and I broadly cover these in other chapters. What I will end with is that while you may feel you have lost a critical part of your identity and memories, I encourage you to focus on what is in front of you today and ahead of you tomorrow. And this is how I found solace in my transition as I realized that one's legacy is not measured by one's professional accomplishments. Your family and friends will not remember what kind of employee you were or how you did your job. They will however, measure your legacy by what you accomplish leaving the world. I discuss this transition further in the chapter GIVING.

THOUGHTS:

DYING

THOUGHTS ON SUICIDAL IDEATION

This is no doubt a very difficult topic to discuss. There are different mindsets you will be in and varying degrees of severity. All of these must be taken seriously and must be addressed. If you are thinking about suicide, at any level, I encourage (implore) you to call the Suicide Hotline at 988.

Personally, I have gone through all of the stages and generally have my arms wrapped around what was going on in my head during those times. This chapter is unique because I have fluctuated between the stages to include attempting suicide twice. The fact I got there, which I will discuss, did not just happen. What I discovered in hindsight is there were many influences driving my actions towards suicide. There were a combination of things that were real and unreal and also things within and outside of my control. The reality is that you could be facing a combination of all of these. They can be overwhelming, both mentally and physically, but they can also cause you complex pain. Not knowing where your thoughts currently are, I want to assure you things can and will get better. This situation can be managed with the right help, possibly medication, as well as changes in your behaviors and actions.

My first thoughts of not wanting to be alive started as a small child. My abusive father literally ruined every aspect of my childhood, but more so, I was terrified of him. As a little boy, I vividly remember him violently raging, and viewing his behavior through my adult eyes now, it seems quite peculiar as it was often over very minor things. Like a petulant child, he would scream, throw and break things. My mother would feebly push back, typically yelling at him, but I now realize that she too was like a child and was generally defenseless. My mother had mental health issues, most that went undiagnosed and untreated until very late in life, so she was essentially trapped with an abusive husband as her family would not assist her. When he calmed down, both my father and mother would continue as though nothing happened.

However, the fact is something did happen. As a child I felt my spirit was broken, which it was, but in reality my brain was being programmed in the fight or flight mode. Not having the cognitive skills to understand what was going on or how to protect myself, I remained scared, often into a numbing state. After this happens repeatedly, you can become stuck in that state of mind and being, and this manifests as certain behaviors. As a child you are defenseless, and in my case, I will categorize my entire childhood as one of fear and not feeling safe. Not being or feeling safe can follow you for life, and as an adult the experiences can continue to haunt you if they aren't addressed. And while I have blocked out many of the details of my childhood, I cannot forget his behavior. As an adult, I am more pragmatic about it, as I have been blessed with the opportunity to help others because of my struggles and experiences. It also gave me a great guideline how not to be as an adult and father.

If you had an abusive or traumatic experience, the complex feelings that arise are part of your Complex PTSD (aka C-PTSD). There is much material on the diagnosis of this, and I will leave this topic here. There is some value in you having a general academic understanding of this, as it will help you organize your symptoms, pool your thoughts and give you a vocabulary that you can use to communicate with your counselor. What I do, however, want to point out is to get into this mindset. There are layers of PTSD that can start when you are child. You may believe that since you are far away from your childhood, that you have grown past it. The reality is you may have not fully dealt with it.

Of course, by the time I went into the military, I was already primed, and the next traumatic events simply built upon this. By primed, I mean I was predisposed to how I lived in fear, managed my thoughts during fearful events or triggers, and subsequently coped with fear after the event passed. For years, I will tell you I did this poorly. I would, however, come to do some of it better as I healed, but a good amount of it I did not do well enough. As my skills were not generally consistent and balanced, this left me emotionally vulnerable. And if there is any point I want to make, no matter how old you are, your childhood impacts you as an adult. This will need to be part of your healing journey if it is relevant to your life experiences, or it can keep you emotionally vulnerable until you work on them.

My military experience was generally poor. What friends and colleagues have shared with me over a number of decades helped me put this in context. I not only experienced multiple traumatic events, but I was in a structure where I feel the chain of command was compromised. Meaning, our chain of command had weak leaders who created or fostered a highly hostile environment due to their poor or weak behaviors. This was just not a single boss, but the entire chain of command projected they were poor leaders in how they behaved. It was not possible to use the next person in the chain, as they were as much of a problem as the one you needed to deal with. Possibly this was a factor of the time, but most within my command attributed this to much deeper issues. Of course, this created a situation where I never felt safe at varying levels. This was a mirror of my abusive father who had absolute power over me.

Again, I felt the overwhelming feeling of being miserable and scared.

During these two phases of my life, meaning my childhood and military service, I never attempted suicide, but I did have suicidal ideations. I did not move into the planning stage, but my life was so miserable that I often wished I wasn't alive. It is not uncommon for all of us to have a fleeting thought of just hating life or having negative thoughts about ourselves. It is, however, not common when the thoughts become extremely negative and their frequency and intensity increases. There is a fine line between those two states of mind, but it comes down to intent and action. And over time, I noticed that line shifting some and in fact, it is not fixed. Some days some things are slightly better, and when something difficult or bad happens you don't react. Some days minor things happen, and it triggers you to those thoughts. If you have been there, you realize how quickly this can change for you and that you go in and out of these thoughts at different paces. This also means you have to understand these scenarios and how you talk yourself down.

Personally, I most commonly wished I just would go to sleep and not wake up. This was periodic, often by what was triggering me in theater, whether battle station, work or watch. What is clear, it became closely tied to sleep, or lack thereof. I was often so exhausted mentally, often to a point of my entire body aching, that I had had enough. In the chapter RESTING, I discuss exhaustion and the necessity to stay on top of this, as best as possible, because the lack of sleep acts like a magnifying glass. And by lack of sleep, I'm not talking about days or weeks, but months or longer. When I attempted suicide the first time, I had not slept well in a couple years. I would pass out from exhaustion and then wake up to nightmares. This left both my mind and my body frail and rattled. I literally hurt to such an extent that my muscles and joints ached all day long.

There was one positive thing during my service that kept me

looking forward. When I've talked to former servicemen, both officers and enlisted, it is hard for some to understand what I experienced, because they had good duty stations and strong leaders. And I'm not talking about combat service here, but I am talking about abusive leadership. For those around me, most of whom were a few years older, they somewhat protected me or they had better life management skills. I often remember the guys talking about the leadership, but at the same time they would mock their behaviors to a point to make us laugh. They also set up a method to warn people when they were coming so all could brace for the inevitable. This helped me some, but not much as I needed. I had a short-timer's calendar and would mark each day off. My many symptoms of depression were strong, though, and I would just obsess on the thought of when I could escape. In today's service and work world, there are ways to deal with this, namely due to the fact of technology making bad behavior of leaders harder to contain. If you are currently in the military or work world and are being abused, you can generally deal with this without retribution, but this absolutely was not the case decades ago.

This does create a contradiction, as you want to be proud of your service, but you may not be proud of what you did, what you experienced, or whom you served with. The military wants to project that it is a great organization, but the reality is it also attracts bad people, like any employer, and when they eventually gain power, they can become poor leaders. This disillusioned me, but also, it was quite disappointing, because it not only tainted my experiences, but made my mental health worse. Looking back on this with much life experience, it is clear how much this impacted my long-term mental health and laid the groundwork for future issues. And over time, I spent much time discussing this trying to rationalize the contradiction of the extremes. It has come down to the fact that I have both good and bad memories. It helped me to understand that it was not a result of my actions or behavior, though at times it possibly could have been, but it was mainly an issue of others' behaviors. That is how trauma transpires. There can be many factors.

There are at least three things that kept me from taking my suicidal ideation to the next level. The first is that I simply did not have an obsession to kill myself. Each day was miserable, but I worked my way through the day to get to the next day. I guess one could simply say "I sucked it up." The second was the fact I was so very busy that I was generally distracted. In high school the ideation was masked by after school activities and homework. In the military it was masked by very long work hours and deployment, and subsequently, in the third phase (my college and post-college) I was just as busy studying and working to pay for it. In each of these phases, I kept myself so busy I didn't have time, and starting with my military service, I embraced the mission-oriented mentality. The third reason I did not take the ideation further, and the most important reason, is that I simply did not have the courage to do it. This is what actually saved me on my first attempt, though my ideation had evolved to a much higher level.

While I had distracted myself by staying overly active, it also meant that I was truly ignoring the reality of my actual mental health. I'm not sure if I fully understood all of the changes that were transpiring, but generally knew that I was not well and was feeling the results of prolonged duress and exhaustion. One could argue that I was faking my wellness to some degree, but I did have a few positive things going on in my life that I felt would pull me out of it. But those few positive things were not enough to outweigh the wave of negative things that would transpire or the subsequent cognitive distortion that would take hold. And this is when my mindset changed toward contemplating suicide, as there were several major life changes occurring at the same time. By life changes I mean moving, new job, new career, and relationship changes. There are others to include illness, injury, death of a loved one, etc. Each of these creates a significant level of stress by itself, but when combined, the amount of stress can exceed one's ability to manage them. And that is where I was. The convergence of so many factors came together and inundated me, and the years of ignoring my mental health rushed out.

Then the real damage began. Where I thought I had been at very high levels of stress in the past, it was probably only a 5 or 6 out of 10. By any measure, that is a great deal of stress, but I never knew anything but stress. What I believe happened is I rationalized that level of stress as normal, but it was not normal by any means. But the fact was that as it unraveled, it just kept getting worse and worse. As details unfolded and as the issues I had masked for decades unraveled, it simply tapped the last amount of life out of me, and there was nobody or anything that could stop the hemorrhaging and collapsing of various pieces of my remaining life. I remember some days thinking as to how the situation could get any worse, or cruel, but it did.

This period of time was simply terrible, but it might have been better had it been for one thing. Specifically, the magnification of the problems stemmed from the fact that I had absolutely no support network. Except for one acquaintance, I literally had nobody else. And I mean nobody. I felt abandoned by so many factors and consequently the other life changes put me in such a very isolated position, meaning geographically, that it blocked any opportunities to get any kind of footing. Had there been more technology, as in cell phones or social media where you can find self-help materials, this might have capped some of the catastrophizing I did. Though understandably warranted, it is with time I've learned how to manage this. If you are at this point now, there are more resources to help you than you might realize. Use them. If someone offers to help you or to be with you. Let them.

At the time and within a mere couple of weeks of having started out a new chapter in life, I found myself and my life completely upside down. I was completely confused, isolated, and even the good parts of my life started disintegrating. It was simply a case that there were so many negative details and influences that they swamped everything else. My entire life was reduced to me, a dark apartment and two cats. It was just an utter mess. I vividly remember gazing into the dark blue walls of the apartment and drifting off for long periods of time.

What transpired over the following months is mostly unclear, though there were a few things that remain. As I was by myself, I did not have any friends or family to clearly assess the situation and guide me. One very close friend I had confided in was subsequently killed in a tragic accident. Sadly, I think he held the key to many topics that would have helped my healing in the future. My sister also came to visit, but I barely remember the details. In later years she noted that I literally looked like I was dying, to include losing significant weight, having a sallow look, and having been completely broken mentally. And that was all the "close" help I had at the time. This lack of detail would later diminish my ability to talk to someone to discuss what they saw in me, the situation and my surroundings. This would have been helpful for my recovery and diagnoses that evolved over many years. I would be headed for a very long and dark journey by myself with little information and very few answers. Many times while talking to a therapist, they would ask about details and I literally had no details about some time periods and events. And now, even decades later, some parts of my memory are wiped clean despite the work and efforts I've made to recover them.

I'm guessing it was for a few months that for all practical purposes I departed reality and had a mental breakdown. I was not diagnosed at the time, but I use it loosely to label that time frame where nearly every independent memory was erased. It was however, a number of years later that a therapist told me that in fact I had a mental breakdown. How I did not end up hospitalized at the time was unclear. It should have happened, however, and if you are offered this, I can't encourage you strongly enough to take advantage of it. Remember, there is no stigma in getting help and more so, if you get the right help, whether counselling or medication in a controlled setting, it can potentially reduce even more trauma. Remember, the aftereffects of trauma can be more trauma, and it can cycle out of control. That is what happened to me.

The first time I attempted to kill myself was by hanging. As I previously noted, I had not slept normally in a couple years. Now mind you, sleep had always been my nemesis. What was different now is "how" I slept. I would not fall asleep as much as pass out from exhaustion. This was further compounded by how I would wake up from night terror, mostly of my military service. I knew my situation was serious and my symptoms severe, but I was lost as to what to do. Keep in mind this was pre-2000 when much less was known about PTSD and, as well, the support services, whether skilled counselors or groups, were not there. As I can recall, the only medication I was ever prescribed at that time was basic anxiety medication, which is pretty mild considering what is available today.

So there I was a complete mess. My life, every aspect of it, was literally in complete shambles. Had I had courage, I most likely would not be writing this. But it would be the fourth stage of my life that started at about age 30 when I found my faith, though that did not stop me from attempting suicide a second time. That time, when my life was incredibly stressful as well, I made one of the dumbest mistakes I have ever made, and that was to stop taking my medication. For some reason I felt I didn't need medication, and by stopping, this gradually put my mindset in a bad place. If you don't think your medication is needed or not working, talk with your doctor and psychiatrist. If you don't like their advice or recommendation, you do have the option of talking to another. I discuss this further in the section HELPING.

How do you know how serious your state of mind is? When I have been at my deepest points in life, I have often found it hard to clarify where I am. Meaning, this falls into the vague questions they often ask, "on a scale of 1 to 5, how do you feel?" Possibly they do this to see how sick you are so they know what action to take, but I question if there is much difference between a 3 and 4 or a 4 and 5. The fact is your rational, mental capacity is diminished and your ability to reason and make sound decisions is not whole. I look back and now understand that when I thought I was a 2 or 3, I was actually higher. Hindsight, though, is useless unless you are using it for the present. You need to find someone with whom you can connect with and who will honestly tell you where they think you are and if you are a risk to yourself. This is not an embarrassing situation, but rather a blessing to start the process of healing and moving forward. It is also why engaging trained mental health and medical professionals as early as possible is so very important.

Earlier, I mentioned there are things you do and don't have control over, and the issue of suicide is one I don't think one fully does. I know I didn't and wish someone had intervened. Had I had a support network or someone nearby to care for me, they would have clued in on this and pushed me toward help. I did not have this, however, and I sank deeper in my malaise. If a close friend or family member comes to you with concerns, do not fake it. It is okay to ask for help, and if you don't ask for help, it may be harder to get it. They may see something in you that you are unable to see yourself.

I want to end this chapter on a positive note. At the time I hit bottom, I could have never foreseen where my life would eventually head. In the chapter GIVING, I found my experiences and general work skills would create opportunities for me to help others. I was so obsessed with the past that I just did not turn around to see the future. While you may not see it now, your experiences, particularly the bad ones, are quite powerful and when properly directed, can have an incredible positive impact on other people. With help and work on your part, things do get better.

THOUGHTS:

FALLING

THOUGHTS ON FLUCTUATING DEPRESSION SYMPTOMS

The original name of this chapter was Depressing, but the more I thought about it, that word implies a steady state. Meaning, one feels depressed, that situation is depressing or one of is suffering depression. It alludes to an unclear and undescriptive state that in reality has a spectrum of intensities that throbs like a torn muscle. In fact, I personally think the word "depression" is pretty much useless due to its inherent complexity. I feel this is well validated, because when entered into an internet search engine, there will be a wide array of results that generalize the symptoms. I have found that there is very little on how it "feels" or how your brain and body are reacting in real time.

When I started writing this book, I wrote notes on various pieces of paper and then organized them by topic. This chapter, by far, had the most notes and it was clear reading them during this project, that I was often in a severe state and grappling to understand what was going on and how to survive. And while I have never been a creative writer, I found the following in my notes from a late Fall morning. "The sun enters the dark stage and the brown, crips leaves lightly applaud. It is another day. A beautiful day. But now the clouds look at me like elongated faces crying in pain. And then it came to me, it is the beginning of another ugly night. A night that will echo with the voices of the past and unknown voices of the coming day. Oh God, why will the night be so long?"

Looking back my diagnosed "depression" was anything but steady and it rolled back and forth from a state of misery to one of being absolutely overwhelmed by a dark, foreboding force. I was not depressed. I was utterly consumed by a myriad of feelings that were all over the place. It was so overwhelming. At times it would literally shut me down and paralyze me to the point I could not physically move. This of course was extremely difficult for me to explain at the time, because I had had no real exposure to therapy and the vocabulary out there was either theoretical or generalized. What I can recall is that every aspect of my inner self was shredded and I was locked in an alternate, dark world with no boundaries. Much like a person in a dark room when the electricity goes out, I was feeling out the walls for the doorway, yet couldn't find it. What I did find were more things that I would trip over.

More so, there were no specific patterns or degrees of intensity, and the symptoms I had one day were not necessarily the same ones I had the next day or days. It was very confusing and coupled with the negative effects, it created this spinning and churning-like feeling. My entire consciousness was being torn apart, and it was the falling of symptoms that kept tearing me apart mentally. And when I say falling, I literally could feel my mind, and sometimes body, declining. One of the best ways to explain this is looking at the amusement ride called Tilt-A-Whirl. If you don't know what it is, search for an image on the internet and it will help you understand the following.

The speed and distance at which I fell during my breakdown remains difficult to measure, but it was the farthest yet in my life. Of course, the only way to measure it is by the length of the recovery time. What only took weeks to unravel me, took several years to grow from. I recall that at times, I felt better, and then when I looked upon those points later, I realized how much that I had continued growing. This would go on for years. It is scary how fast I self-destructed, because I realize that I could end up back there, though it was probably less likely. I now know the signs, how to address them, and have a VA counselor that can help me untangle the mess. What I can say definitively is that when I broke down, I couldn't fall any further and this was truly the first point in my life that I became suicidal.

As you are probably aware, the term depression involves numerous categories and symptoms that impact every aspect of your life including behavior, motivation, cognition, sleep, mood, appetite, and a variety of other feelings. Each one of these has a list of symptoms below them. So if you can imagine the Tilt-A-Whirl, imagine two to three symptoms in each car and the car is spinning and going up and down as the entire ride spins. So like the car, each symptom can morph as it spins, meaning its exact feeling changes, and the intensity can increase or fall like the car does. For me, that is why my worst bouts of depression were so hard to explain. Some days behavior and motivation were lower, while my cognition had stabilized a bit. A day or so later, that equation changed as noted in the imagery above.

This chapter is filled with imagery that comes from journaling during the early years. Many of my notes expressed the difficulty of explaining it as I could not wrap my head around how vast and complex my thoughts had become. The explanations were more than words and more so, I used analogies to describe the feelings and the world I was living in.

And it would be the key word "world" that I used often. In one note it discusses me living in two parallel worlds, one that is real and the other that isn't. Both worlds have positive and negative forces, and while we mostly live in the real world, the line between the two is very thin and fragile. The unreal world is where depression thrives. A world where the brain plays tricks on you creating fantasy and dreams, but really cognitive distortions, pain and sometimes horror. And while I had not given up fully, the danger became that my unreal world was dwarfing the real one and eventually the unreal world became the real one. This is much like driving down a highway and noticing you had gone several miles and were not sure how you got there. My entire life had become that way. In fact, I am utterly amazed how I functioned and survived at all. This dual world would never go away enough that I would forget it and I discuss this in the chapter DRIFTING.

I believe that I have experienced these symptoms since I was a child, though my earliest memories are mostly gone, I do have one. I recall as a little boy sitting on the steps leading to the second floor of our house and looking into the blank wall wishing I was dead. My uncle saw me and asked if I was ok, and replied that I was. But the reality is I wasn't. In hindsight, I wish someone had intervened as that laid the groundwork for untreated depression well into my adulthood. But as anyone who reads this knows, there is a stigma regarding this illness, which in itself precludes so many from getting help or conversely helping someone who does.

The one thing that so vividly stands out is when I finally mentally broke down, it was a very rapid decline and like falling, you are well aware of the direction you are headed, but you can't stop it. When I reviewed my notes, there was a common theme of being overwhelmed by so many symptoms, which I noted before were changing in intensity. But combined, these symptoms created a situation where I lost a great deal of control over my life and a degree of pain that was dwarfing the normal functions of life. I will discuss that further, though they of course will be different intensities for each person. One's senses, thoughts and behaviors can become distorted, some created by the illness and others created by yourself in response to them.

Clearly, if you have been dealing with this long enough, you most likely will be able to articulate what you are feeling. If you are new to the healing journey, hopefully some of the things I have experienced will help you put to words what you are feeling. While I discuss this in the chapter LEARNING, I want to touch on it again here. Because of the complexity of the symptoms, if you have a counselor, they should be helping you draw out what you are "really" feeling in lieu of talking in generalities. These conversations should be thorough and should include the intensity and combinations of them based on the time of day and specific triggers. As an example, as I talk about in the chapter CUTTING, there were certain things and people that made me feel worse and often rapidly.

The overall situation that my life was in really was not good, and both my physical and mental wellness were even worse. Understandably, when so many things in your life are bleak, it is very easy to fall into a negative mode. This happens to all of us, but the real problem becomes when you become stuck and for a long period of time. My guess is this builds upon your fight or flight responses, which is your safeguard to protect you. I became cynical about much of everything. My trust of people and the world was very low, causing me to question most things that came before me. And subsequently, I then struggled to find happiness in everything internally and externally, even though there were some good things happening in my life. We often refer to this as a "bitter person," but my behavior was different. I simply did not trust anyone and I didn't know how to. My brain distorted all situations and when coupled with all the other symptoms I had, I was trapped in my world trying to survive.

The first situation that occurred was the distortion of time and in some cases, I lost a complete sense of time. We all face this when we are sick, but I found this really magnified during my worst mental health periods. Like a runner that hits a wall, your mind and body in conjunction with one another shut down, unless you are able to power through it. And when your mind is totally out of kilter, it probably isn't possible. From my notes, I saw that the concept of minutes and hours was gone, and the time distortion coupled with pain created a situation where my frame of mind was dragging and time was elongating. Meaning, when one becomes so exhausted, it seems that time is going slower, as in looking at a clock and just waiting for your shift to be over. Instead, time had evolved to a much broader measurement of day and night, as in light or dark, and even more broadly to on and off, though technically, the amount I was shut off was very little. More so, my nights were very long and, metaphorically, far more dark. This is when my mind would begin to magnify thoughts and create an array of cognitive distortions.

It would be many years later that I would learn how much sleep impacts your well-being. This seems self-explanatory, but in context to when I broke down, I did not have access to very good counselling and from what I recall, it was closer to getting help from a PCP. As I recall, I was given pills for anxiety and that was it. The situation of course is far more complex and needs multiple approaches at the same time. For some, sleep may become a coping tool to heal the damaged brain and body, but this was not the case for me. In fact, sleep, or lack thereof, would eventually become one of my most significant symptoms.

My notes show I simply didn't sleep well at all, if I even really slept. In one comment, which was three years after my breakdown, I wrote in depth that I didn't fall asleep as much as passing out from exhaustion. Conversely, I didn't wake up, but was thrusted into a panic state after being awoken from night terror. As the years progressed, I managed to fall asleep much easier, but did not stay asleep. For over two decades, I would get a maximum of five to six hours of sleep a night, but that time was not usually connected. Eventually, and after years of therapy and psychiatrists, they found a medication that would give me six to seven hours of consecutive sleep. For some this might not seem enough, but I was thrilled and it worked well enough. Regarding the night terror, that continued solidly for a decade. I was blessed to have a caring wife who had a nursing background and she would help me manage it and get me back to sleep. And I can't thank her enough as I know my flailing arms, screaming and crying were unnerving to her, but she put my care first.

From a physical perspective, my body was not just taking a beating from the mental health issues and fatigue, it was deteriorating from not eating. And that has not fully changed as I have found that when my mental health is off, that I lose the interest to eat. I remember at one point, though I didn't mark the date, I looked into the mirror and saw a dying man. And this in itself fed into me wanting to die and for whatever rationalizations I had at the time, it did not seem important enough to me. Years later, my sister brought this to my attention and shared the concern she had. Apparently, though I am 5'6" and have always been somewhat fit, I had probably lost no less than 20% of my body weight based on the description as how my clothes were hanging on my body and couldn't tighten my belt as much as I needed too.

Fast forward to this point in life, I still lose interest to eat when my mental health is not at 100%. I'm not sure why this is and why this remains a significant symptom when I am so aware of it. More so, when I don't eat, I typically don't feel hunger pains even when I don't eat for a day. Food just does not seem appealing and possibly it is subconsciously the energy it takes to produce it that deters me to some degree. Of course, I realize this is not healthy, but I have a keen awareness and have learned to press myself to eat whether I want to or not. Fortunately, having a caring wife, it is probably one of the more common things she asks me, "What have you eaten today?" If this is an issue for you and if you just don't feel like eating, be honest with both your doctor and counselor. To supplement my diet, and also because of surgery I had on my jaw while in the service that impacts what I can eat, I drink supplement shakes and take multi-vitamins. It goes without saying if you don't eat it is going to make this overall situation worse.

My behavior was significantly impacted. I know it influenced how I answered and interacted with people, but in itself this created another issue of desiring isolation. I am both an internalizer, as in stuffing my feelings, and an isolator, the latter which is so significant in my life. Isolation is such a significant portion of my life that I have given it its own chapter ISOLATING. This is important, as I know I minimized my time with other people, and when I did, I was very careful who it was. For those I spent more time with, like at work, I really had to guard what I said, because my head was filled with so many thoughts, many of which were negative. My behavior at the time no doubt projected sadness and anger, by my emptiness and at times hopelessness, all created a level of pessimism. And unfortunately, and regretfully, I became a more negative person than I wish I had.

Motivation is another area that effects some people much more than others. I would later be categorized as having high-functioning depression, meaning that I was able to perform my general daily routine or tasks. In speaking with fellow veterans, I have noticed many who were able to do this well. My belief is that may be from military training which teaches you stay on the "mission" at any cost. In fact, looking at all that I was going through, I am absolutely surprised I could do my job at all in the first few years; though admittedly, much of those details were wiped out along with the bad memories. Fast forward decades, I still had this ability, but I was quite aware that despite me overloading my body, I kept powering through the days as I had no choice. My mission was to care for my family, and in many ways I wish I had the ability to get a much less stressful job and life situation. As I am now retired, I can see how that damaged me and stole many good things away from my life, which I am now trying to recover.

My current stability, while generally good, is periodically taxed and there are certain influences when I can feel the falling effect. Those are mostly environmental factors including, time of day, temperature and light. For most of my life, I have generally been a morning person. When it is late in the day, and particularly after a day where I worked hard and am tired, I can feel this tugging at me. Having a routine, as in how you close down the day or prepare for bed, is crucial to keeping you on track. The most significant thing I do is try to consistently take my night-time medication and go to sleep about the same time each evening. I notice when I don't, I feel this more the next day.

The two other factors that really impact me are the light, as in when the sun goes down or comes up. This parallels the Fall and Winter months, and I can literally feel the energy being squeezed out of my body. This is further coupled with acute days of cold or significant daily temperature swings. They now call this SAD (Seasonal Affective Disorder), and this has to be managed before it kicks in. For myself, I also have issues of extreme heat outside and this in itself can cause me to dissociate or cause me to become anxious as it takes me back to my Middle East days. If you have environmental factors that impact you, you will need a plan to manage them and keep yourself grounded. In cold weather, I like to wear layers of clothes and mentally set goals early in the day that give me a level of achievement. These approaches subsequently keep me moving. In the Summer, I move slower and methodically, breathe through my nose and drink lots of water. If I am feeling too much anxiety, I find a cooler place, practice breathing exercises and take a break.

This of course all comes from a common theme where I have a pre-planned strategy of positive skills. Each morning, whether I think I need to or not, I think through my forthcoming day and what could impact my stability. My wife would implant one phrase that has had a profound impact and it is "what are you grateful for today?" This is profound, because it forces you out of the victim or sickness mode and into the survivor or functioning mode. This very approach will help you cope and battle your foreboding symptoms or tasks ahead. And while I still have these factors that influence my behavior, I ask myself regularly "is this real or is this unreal, can I control this or can't I control this?" This is somewhat similar to the Serenity Prayer, but it is quicker to practice and embed into your response mechanism. What I eventually learned is that I was a survivor. Being a victim, which is real, is a very difficult place to recover from when you are falling. If you learn to be a survivor, you will learn to monitor and manage your symptoms when you are falling. To that, I am quite keen on how my body and mind are at equilibrium. When I feel changes coming, I acknowledge them and put into practice the correct skills to manage them.

As you begin to monitor or manage your symptoms, it is the falling symptoms, not the rising ones, you need to observe. Each day I review in both the morning and afternoon the following: energy, happiness, relaxation, calmness, and clarity. You of course can add others, but these five words best describe where I want my mind to be. These are the counterbalance to my falling symptoms.

You may choose to enter this in a table format or simply write it in a daily journal. Whatever approach you use, make sure you are comfortable with it and that it is both repeatable and sustainable. I typically do this late morning when my mind is fully engaged and early evening before I become tired. Another thing I monitor is the speed of how fast my mood and attitude decline, meaning was it gradual or fast. As noted before, this is sometimes inconsistent for me, but this gives me important information to discuss with my counselor. This is a bit of work and will require commitment, but I assure you that having embraced this, it has really aided the management of my PTSD.

THOUGHTS:

FEELING

THOUGHTS ON NEGATIVE OR ABSENT FEELINGS

The greatest challenge I have faced with my feelings is when I'm at my worst, I am swamped with many at the same time and at my best, they have evaded me to the point that I in an emotionally numb state. And that is how it is with PTSD, often too much or too little. We can intensely feel many things for periods of time, often when we don't want to and they can seem to be illogical for what we should be feeling. Conversely, we know we should be feeling things at certain times, yet we feel absolutely nothing and sometimes to the point that we feel numb. This altered response to life can leave us both confused and fatigued.

While there are of course many feelings, the one that probably impacts those with PTSD the most is love. Depending on the type of trauma you suffered, feeling loved or being able to love is very difficult. We expect a certain level of love from family, and we may never find it. We expect a certain level of love from partners or spouses, and it may change over time. But we are also burdened by our own fears and insecurities, which may keep love from flourishing, even when it is before us. Our brain tells us things that may or may not be real and subsequently, we awkwardly try to manage them. Finding love is difficult by its own merits, but PTSD can make it a very difficult, even mythical place we can't seem to find. It may seem at times that you will never find love or it may not find you.

Most of my childhood remains a blur, though there are some memories, mostly unpleasant. And now having much hindsight and wisdom to reflect, I can reasonably say that it was an unfortunate and dark time in my life. A damaged childhood is ultimately the most difficult part of one's life to come to terms with. It is the pre-you of who you have become and the foundation of almost every aspect of how you think and behave. And as you age, it is hard to address as layers of other issues and dysfunction are built upon it as well. Your memory can't recall all of the pieces that tie it together and your current thoughts may be askew.

For myself, living under an oppressive and abusive father, his behaviors clouded most everything good that did or could have happened throughout my entire childhood. At home we all constantly walked on eggshells, as we never knew what insignificant situation would throw him into a violent tirade. As singing was his hobby, his deep base voice coupled with extreme power was absolutely frightening. And when it began, there was no place to hide in our small house, and the only way to escape it was to wait for it to end. Sometimes it was yelling and tantrums. Many times it was just verbal abuse.

As a child, I was, of course, defenseless. And his behaviors and the dysfunctional household tore me apart from the earliest age. From the age of about 5, as I have no recollection of the time prior, I never remember him not acting out and I never remember not being afraid of him. In other words, I never saw a normal state in my home. My sister, who was four years my senior, told me in later years she sheltered me from much of it which I found astonishing. I didn't think it could get worse, but it obviously did for her. I have vague recollections of him hitting her on a few occasions, but it was more common than I was aware. My mother, who was small and feeble, had little resilience against him besides yelling back at him. But she lost and we also lost, as she subsequently, did not protect us adequately. And as she was fully enabled, and incapable in a number of ways, she obliged us to remain in the abuse. And so it continued relentlessly as we were all bullied and controlled in every aspect of our life. All of our moves were calculated in such a way to prevent him from acting out or avoiding him when he did.

Looking back, I can say that from my earliest memories, I never felt loved at any level by any member in my immediate or extended family, except by my sister. That was limited, as she was four years older, and by the time she was in high school, she had found her own avenues of escape. More so, I don't recall nurturing by my mother, which I would come to understand in later years. Looking back, this is really incomprehensible, even considering her shortcomings. I knew things were very wrong and the constant hurt I was feeling was not normal. But that is all I ever experienced and my only exposure to affection was watching how friends' parents interacted with their children or between themselves. As I made a conscientious decision at a very young age to stay away from my parents, I at least recognized that there was normalcy beyond my family.

Our house was either in a neutral or anger state. It was the calm before the storm. There was seldom happiness created in our family, except possibly when my parents were drinking or in public, but that was usually a performance. I would hear decades later from high school friends and people in the community how nice my parents were. Of course I wanted to tell them the truth, but I guess that was not their truth. But it amazed me how my father was able to hide the person he was, though this book reveals it.

During my childhood, I have no recollection of seeing my parents being affectionate towards one another. I never saw them hold hands, kiss or doing anything romantic, as is the case with close couples. All other positive emotions were also nearly void in all aspects of my family life and to me, and those that I experienced were negative or acted-out. So instead, the concept of positive emotion was missing, and I found myself focused on how I could get away from them. In the simplest of terms, it was as if my sister and I were adopted by clueless adults who did not like one another.

But unknowingly, the lack of such love had a lasting effect on me, through my formative years and well into my adulthood. Instead, it was survival, stability and success that I placed value on. Everything I did and all my interactions were self-centered with the objective of escaping and moving forward. My first period of escape was about five years old, once school started. To keep this in context, the period of the late 1960s, kids left home and played all day and returned home when the streetlights turned on. I astutely realized that I could go to my friend's house, or play away from home, for most of the time outside of school hours. And so I would actually do this until I went into the service.

In place of love and affection, I had to create my own positive emotions and feelings, which I did by acting out and creating situations at which to laugh. So at a fairly young age, I found out that I was somewhat clever at doing pranks and also smart enough not to telescope them. And because my school grades generally remained in the B to C range, I was able to use this as a shield. As I could also keep a straight face at the right time, I don't think people fully connected them too me. But in hindsight, while this brought me a way to relieve the tension in my life, this also created my personality. Some thought it was funny no doubt, but I also know it created some animosity towards me. And while I stopped the pranks mostly when I left home, my attitude remained and so it clearly kept people from liking me and, potentially, others from loving me.

The other aspect of not feeling loved is that my mind remained in a constant state of escape, sometimes dreamful, and eventually in difficult times suicidal. I never really had big dreams, but I was a dreamer. I spent much time thinking about an alternate life, namely one that was happy. But of course, the latter was common, depending on my emotional state, and it increased with frequency. And while some might not comprehend how a child could think of suicide, the concept is easy and practical. Probably by the time I was 5 or 6, I wanted life to end.

And suicide is sadly one string of memories that I vividly recall. I remember being crawled up in a ball or sitting quietly in a sheltered space just trying to understand what to do and where to go. I remember moments of being alert and shortly thereafter crashing into a state of gnawing gloom. And often I would just sit there wondering why I couldn't just die. So many days I just wanted to turn life off. Yet somehow, I survived the oppression, as agonizing and unbearable as it was. But the foundation of depression, as well as the thoughts to die would continue well into my adulthood and be the underpinnings of my PTSD.

By the time I was 12 or 13, I was exposed to both alcohol, almost always beer, and marijuana. As my friends and I had older friends, this gave us access to it. For me, these both were miracles. For the first time in my life, I found an absolute escape from the brutality I was living under and I embraced it heavily. No matter how difficult my current situation was, I could imbibe in these and quickly slip away from reality into a generally peaceful, though disorganized state.

Beer was my first real experience of outright intoxication. I recall being a young freshman in high school getting a six pack and drinking the entire thing. At that moment, sip by sip, I could feel the sadness and anxiety lifting. And as I progressed from bottle to bottle, I would slip into a passive and lethargic state of numbness. This was such an incredible feeling. One of being free, quiet and alone.

But marijuana would ultimately become my favorite. I could feel myself in a somewhat normal way, but was not incapacitated in the same way as alcohol. This alternate world became my first controllable escape from the mental abuse. Any time I was feeling crushed, I could quickly create an exit from reality. By the time I was 14 or 15, I was drinking heavily at least once a week and smoking marijuana almost daily. I would just sit there weaving in and out of reality but fully enjoying the lift of my burdens. This scene would repeat regularly and for a number of years and during my non-school hours, I might have been under the influence 30-40% of the time. It was my world which I controlled. It was a strange world, but it was mine and I felt safe within it.

So as other kids were beginning the process of socializing and dating, I was self-absorbed in my personal world. I had one objective and that was to survive the abuse and plan an exit strategy from my childhood home. Though of course in hindsight it was not the right thing to do, but it most certainly was far better than the reality I was experiencing. And honestly, I don't believe I had any other options at the time. There was nobody to talk too, whether a teacher, neighbor or one of my few relatives. Nobody knew of my torment, which decades later I would find out not to be the case. They just chose not to get involved. Whether right or wrong, alcohol and drugs kept me from hurting or killing myself. This, of course, laid the false groundwork that emotions and feelings were not needed for survival.

This period of my life was subsequently the first phase and the foundation to layers of PTSD that would be the hardest to recover from. The succinct set of issues, all of which are complex, I would be required to acknowledge and address decades later. And it is for that reason I spend so much time in my writing discussing this period of my life and how I broke these issues into manageable pieces so I could acknowledge and make adjustments. And this is important. PTSD is often not the singular and obvious event that we want to easily label as the cause of our issues. It is often predisposed by one or more events or by a period of time in one's life.

And it will take multiple strategies and tactics to tackle it. If you have PTSD, it is quite possible you have layers of PTSD.

So as an adult, with my first failed marriage behind me and my life crash landing, I suffered a breakdown. Much of that time is blurred, but I do remember how confused and unsure I was. Over the next few years as I gained some stability, I happened upon a number of things that positively influenced me and the potential direction of my life. I knew I had to make corrections and was willing to do so. It wasn't until I happened upon an article talking about the statistics for those who remarry, that it really registered how important these changes be made. I don't recollect the exact numbers, but basically recall that each sequential time you get married, the chances of it failing increase, as well. It meant that I would really have to take full ownership and deal with all aspects of my life. It also meant I would have to come to terms as to what love really was and how to achieve a deep lasting love with a future wife.

While I will discuss in other chapters many aspects of the corrections I made to get me to this point, I do want to discuss two succinct things that I discovered to ensure my relationship with my wife would succeed. The first and most important thing that aided our success was the mutual commitment we accepted. We both embraced our oaths seriously and without hesitation knew this was final. There were going to be no excuses, no burdens, no interferences that would dissolve our relationship. Years later, we both agree this was a cornerstone to our success. My wife is my best friend, and I realize how fortunate I am to have met her.

The second thing that was revealed is that love is learned. Early on in my career, I asked an Indian coworker about his arranged marriage. I was intrigued as to how his parents picked his wife, how long he was married, and how he achieved happiness. I asked him "how was your marriage so successful?" He gave me multiple reasons to include his faith, his culture, and the respect for his parent's selection. But it was the fourth thing he said that stood out and was ultimately one of the best pieces of advice I have ever been given. I asked him "did you not love her before you married?" He responded "you grow to love each other."

For the first time in my life, I had a plan to create love, embrace love and come to know what it was. I knew that I had been blessed by my wife, but this gave me hope that not only could I improve how I love her, but I could also improve how I love myself. This in turn would create an environment that her love for me would grow and would forever bind us together. And thirty years later, I can say it worked and that the approach "grow to love" is a strategy that can be used by those who have PTSD. What I believe happened is some of the perceived myths about relationships, as well as some superfluous relationship rituals, were tempered. This is not to say we did not experience things that many young couples do, but that we hastened our path to building a stronger and lasting relationship.

Some say marriage is hard work. I would argue that marriage requires constant awareness and effort particularly when you have PTSD. You are obliged to be aware and manage many feeling and behaviors that probably come more naturally for those that don't suffer from PTSD. And it is not big things that make a marriage succeed, but small repetitive things that are subtle and utilized in our daily routine. Kind, simple words and positive acknowledgements are building blocks. This of course includes saying "I love you."

With many years of marriage, I do love my wife increasingly more. My love, respect and adoration for her are truly impenetrable. I am absolutely indebted to her. At times I just stand afar and quietly watch her. I think about us, what we have been through together and who we are as people now. I think about all of the distractions and difficulties of life. They are just that, and they come and go. Material possessions, money, health, friends, etc. all come and go. Our relationship and love for each other has not gone. And

I am continuing to understand what it means to love and to be loved.

The effects of your PTSD symptoms are strong and for myself, near constant, even a number of decades out. This is just like the phases of your life where you feel good about it, or not, so does your ability to love. If you are feeling depressed or overwhelmed, it is hard to muster the strength or focus on loving another. And even though I know I should act and feel in a certain way, I do find that I have to remind myself to be loving.

There will be times that you may become emotionally numb to the point you can't feel, identify or display some emotions. I was in the most severe state of emotional numbness after my breakdown, but it subsided as I progressed improving many aspects of my life. Admittedly though, it still briefly comes and goes to this day, but typically for short durations.

PTSD can also create a mindset that you are worthless, ugly and not deserving of love. This of course is your brain tricking you. You are worthy and deserving of love, but there has to be a willingness to make changes in your life so you can experience it. If you have shortcomings, you know what they are. If you have triggers, you will need to establish boundaries. If you aren't caring for your broader self, you will need to improve your self-care. If you are struggling to point your basic function is impeded, you will need to work with your doctor, your counselor, and support group. I mention all of these things as your strategy will require you to address multiple areas simultaneously and consistently. It is a great deal of effort, but it is all part of your path forward to regaining your feelings and emotions. The chapters ACCEPTING, CUTTING, HELPING, and UNDERSTANDING delve into these further.

What I discovered is no matter where you are in your journey, you have a clean slate to change any aspect of your life including who you are, where you are headed and how you act. In my case when I made this decision, I was not worried about making mistakes, because my life was an absolute mess, and the changes I made could only make it better. Some things worked and some things didn't, but overall I refocused my life. Looking back many years later, I am grateful of the changes I made. And while it may seem mechanical per se, you have to practice the changes like any other habit. In a sense, you are going to have to learn how to feel emotions and love again. At first, it was awkward for me, and I felt as though I was faking it and wasn't being honest with myself. At other times, it seemed futile and difficult, because after some time I still wasn't feeling anything from my changes, though it was the regular challenges of life that were distracting me from many levels of feelings, not just love. The reality however was the changes were taking hold and I was becoming more of the person I wanted to be. It was subtle at times, but I saw my interaction and response by people was becoming more favorable.

And with decades behind me, I know when I look at my wife and kids, I love them and they love me. This validates the fact that no matter how much trauma one has been through, that feeling love is a possibility. And that is the hope for those with PTSD. You are worthy of love and you are capable of loving, though you may have to learn and practice it over some time to make it happen. What you may also find is that once you begin finding and displaying love, that many of the other feelings fall in behind.

THOUGHTS:

FORGETTING

THOUGHTS ON MEMORY AND MEMORIES

It would be several years into my healing when I would come to the realization that the sharpness of my mind was not going to rebound to its peak of my college days. That is not to say that I was no longer sharp or capable of profound thinking, but the way my brain was working had changed. It is difficult to recall when it first began to start, but it was slow at first, then appeared to happen in plateaus. Meaning it worsened over time and compounded in stages. Of course, as you age there are generally accepted memory changes, but this was not the same. This was also coupled with my mind flickering like an old light bulb, which I cover in the chapter DRIFTING.

For those who go through trauma, your brain may not only rewire itself, but it may alter your thought processes moving forward. The changes in my brain were subtle at first, and I attributed them to me being very busy with work and life. In fact, life was moving forward at a rapid pace. In just a few years I had married, moved to another part of the country and had two beautiful sons to care for. While the focus on my life was still important, particularly my career, it was no longer the dominant factor. Caring for my wife and kids was. As my wife didn't work outside of the home, it required more diligence and time on my part to ensure we had an adequate income. This is not too different than many families, and it obliged me to travel for work where pay is typically higher. At its peak, I was in a hotel about 80 nights a year, sometimes more and sometimes less. When I came home for the week, I was understandably tired and let some details in life slip.

What I would come to realize many years later was that the changes were far more complex than I was aware of. I would come to understand how PTSD can have a significant impact on both your present thinking and memories of the past. As I continued counseling and support groups, I would learn new concepts and hear others speak of varying types of memory loss. From what I was hearing and reading, I was probably somewhere in the middle, but as noted, my deterioration was worse than I realized.

My many years with PTSD have adversely impacted my memory, and I will attempt to explain the many forms in which it has materialized. Conceptually, the most prevalent issue is that it impacted what I remembered from my past. I found a myriad of recollections from my past were illogically embedded in my memory. In order to gain an understanding of my past, I segmented my life into the following eras: childhood, military, college, premarriage, and married (with children). As I had trauma in multiple of those areas, it gave me the chance to tackle specific issues within each time era.

But what came to surprise me is what I did not remember, and it was no small amount of people, places and things that I had forgotten. Specifically, I estimate that I suppressed probably 90% or more of all memories up until my current marriage. And this most certainly wasn't because of effort and approaches. In therapy sessions, counselors and doctors would ask questions and I would simply have a blank memory. This loss of memory was not just bad experiences, but all experiences. The only way I discovered information was by asking my older sister and a few close friends who would fill me in. But even that did not help, as they would give me very accurate and detailed information; yet I would still have no recollection of my involvement. In some cases there were pictures of me, and when looking at them, I couldn't rationalize what was transpiring, as I had no recollection of how or when they were taken. This has happened so many times that I have come to accept that my life is mostly comprised of my present-day life.

I guess there is both an upside and downside to this. Not recalling bad events can help one move forward as you won't dwell upon the past. But at the same time, it can also keep you from fully understanding what created your triggers and symptoms. Hence this can conversely keep you from moving forward. For myself, when I reviewed my notes and diaries, I found myself writing about a person I didn't always fully know. While of course I wrote those thoughts, I didn't recall writing them, which obliged me to stitch the details together in order that I could paint a broader picture. In some ways it was like writing a biography of another person. Some of what I would read was profoundly sad. Some of it was philosophical rambling, but at times there were snippets of hope. Possibly this unmarred approach is what permitted me to write so pragmatically from both the heart and experience. With the therapy I had had, I could understand my mindset or at least what I was trying to articulate in part.

That said, amnesia can be a very real part of PTSD and impacts people in different ways. Over time, I am surprised how much that I have really forgotten, particularly the good things that happened in my life. For the simplicity of explaining the broader changes, my life can be split into two time periods, with the better one being after my marriage. As I move into this latter period, my wife of nearly thirty years is my best friend and has always had my best interests in mind. She has been crucial in my decades of healing and life of many positive experiences that we have shared together. But my memory of that has also been impacted at times, though I remember a great deal more than the earlier part of my life. And yes, with some gentle reminders, she often refreshes my memories of other things. As I like to tell her, "I get to enjoy some things three or four times!"

A serious issue, or I should say condition or disorder, that falls under memory is night terror. I suffered horribly from this prior to my marriage and at least five years into it. The terror was significant, and while there typically were a core of repeating story lines, including those that were real and unreal, most had me in scenarios of extreme duress or danger. Those from the Middle East were particularly pronounced, and I guess much of it was releasing in my sleep as I worked to avoid the triggers during the day. In response, I often awoke screaming, crying, sweating and thrashing. Many times I would snap out of the terror by entering reality with a full panic attack, short of breath and aching. Other times my wife would gently pull me out of them and then coax me back to sleep. And unlike a bad dream, I would also wake up confused and unable to recall many of the actual details, though often my body and mind felt like I had just been in the thick of it. Over time, I took enough notes that I was able to understand the story lines so I could discuss them with a counselor.

This is one part of your memory that you wish you would forget, and many like myself are plagued with it for years. I would estimate that this was a significant issue for shy of fifteen years. Yet over time it did decline to the point where it was infrequent. I still have them, but seldom at this point. What helped me reduce them was a number of things. Firstly, with the Veterans Administration (VA), I began receiving the right type of therapy to include trauma-focused therapy, group therapy, and self-education, such as books and videos. For a while, I took a medication that helped reduce it as well. But in hindsight, possibly one of the key strategies I embraced was to reduce many triggers in my life that caused much of the anxiety that I often brought to bed. I removed many things and people from my life, which I discuss in the chapter CUTTING. Over decades, the strategies that I embraced significantly reduced the level of my anxiety and subsequently, my learned skills were capable of managing the remainder of them. While I still have night terror infrequently, I have developed steps to bring myself down when I awake. I also had extreme nightmares, but they too lessened over time and in the present day are often just bizarre content leaving me to think "I wonder what that means?"

Another serious issue that impacts those with PTSD is panic attacks. While they occurred at various times and with different intensities, my attacks fell into a few categories. Firstly, my attacks were triggered by those things my family did in my past and were reactivated by either them or others who acted similarly. This of course subsided to some degree when I stopped contact with these types of people. From my military service, the attacks fell into a specific type of images, namely from the Middle East, as well as very specific smells. This, too, subsided with counseling but also embracing positive behaviors like not watching certain types of movies or news programs. One type of panic attack that would occur, though seldom, is where I was not aware of what was causing it. Meaning, I would be functioning normally, and it would just happen. This is unnerving and most certainly causes confusing distress. It is hard to eliminate all of the triggers that cause them, but if you put a lot of needless things into your brain, such as movies or computer games, it can back up and come out as pain. But over time, the number and intensity of panic attacks lessened. The key thing is to be aware of your triggers and learn how to manage them.

The next group of memories are what I would categorize as general, random memories. Despite being hypervigilant to avoid certain things that trigger you, there is no possible way of stopping all of them. For myself, these memories would randomly come to mind often for no specific reason. And this is where having learned skills to manage them is crucial. I found that I could be in the middle of an average day and a past, bad memory would come up without any apparent trigger. While I have a generalized anxiety disorder and have a tendency to lean towards a state of hypervigilance, these innocuous events would readily amplify my anxiety. This is different than the magnitude of a panic attack and you may simply feel tightness in your throat or chest. While I think you can better manage these in off hours, this will take preparation in public settings, particularly work. Some of the memories may be quite debilitating, yet you may not be afforded the privacy to come down from them in a subtle manner. In later years, a couple of colleagues, who would come to learn of my military service, noted how they were perplexed at times by my quirky behaviors. Without doubt, they saw me adjusting my behavior publicly. Though I thought I was containing my reactions, some of it in fact was projecting subtly. And this is what needs to be managed as you move forward. I discuss this in the chapter UNDERSTANDING.

Without question, anyone with PTSD wonders when the ugliness subsides. I use this word as this myriad of thoughts is so utterly complex and often dark. And after an extensive period of time, you just want it to stop invading your mind and present experiences. But again, this takes a great deal of effort on your part and learning how to reframe your present experiences. There is no simple approach or answer and it very well may take years of therapy and practice. In speaking with many people over the years and comparing experiences, it does lessen not only with time but embracing sound behavioral practices. As I am over 60 now, I found that certain skills I learned and strategies I employed did not fully stop the bad memories, but it most certainly reduced the number of triggers and subsequently allowed me to address them more quickly and efficiently. I also realize that had I had certain types of therapy with the right individuals earlier, the duration and intensity of my healing would not have taken the time it did.

The number one source of triggers will most likely be people, because of how they act or even react to you. As both of you can feed into the interaction, this can escalate the communication, and it can elevate the intensity and content of the rest of the dialogue. If you have PTSD, you are obliged more than the average person to control your behavior. The other may or may not know of your situation and, more so, may or may not care. It needs to be decided whether or not you will continue the relationship with them, whether it be a family member, friend or co-worker. While it is one's first reaction to make things work, the element of PTSD is a much different variable that necessitates some absolute changes. One's PTSD is not going to go away and only dedication to working on it will prevail. If a person continues triggering you, you have a choice of establishing boundaries or going as far as ending the relationship. It may require greatly reducing or completely eliminating contact with a family member. This is not an easy thing to implement and I cover my thoughts about this in the chapter CUTTING.

A particularly difficult relationship is one where you are obliged to interact or communicate with someone who caused your trauma. This namely falls into the category of family or possibly a former partner. Those people who fall outside of that realm are easier to detach from and could possibly already be gone. In my instance, having a relationship with my parents and others who impacted me was not possible. And this is where forgiveness comes in.

Personally, I find the concept of forgiveness to be a loaded term. The word is usually used in two contexts, those being religious and therapeutic. The religious one is fairly well known, so I won't go into depth of it here, but it essentially obliges the offended to forgive their perpetrator. This approach allows one to "spiritually" release oneself from the past. The therapeutic is mostly the same and suggests if you take certain steps, it will permit you to "mentally" leave your past behind and move forward. While on the surface both of these seem admirable, it may not be either pragmatic or realistic with those with PTSD. And that is simply because your brain has been rewired and will continue to attempt to make you think in a certain way.

For those who have been in trauma, there is a desire for forgiveness to have an element of reconciliation. Specifically, there is an avenue for you to address the person(s) who caused you great strife and it gives them an opportunity to acknowledge or apologize to you. Understandably, this is an ideal scenario as the trauma impacted your life both significantly and permanently. It provides a degree of validation and more importantly, some level of closure. And by closure, I mean it stops the ongoing thoughts and memories that continue when this does not happen.

While I have no understanding of how often this happens, from my personal discussions over multiple decades, this does not happen very often. I have heard of a few instances where this has occurred, with a couple of them being fairly significant acts, but generally it heads in the wrong direction to denial, avoidance, gaslighting or even retaliation. Hence, if you have already sustained extreme duress from the past, this can simply trigger, or even worse, exacerbate the past trauma further. It will just cause another layer of harm and a string of additional bad memories.

This is what happened with my family and as I better understood psychological concepts from therapy, I understood what I was up against. In the simplest of terms, I was attempting to have a rational conversation with irrational or irresponsible people. The worst of the purposeful interactions is gaslighting, as the family member often knows what your trigger buttons are, as they installed them. Also, if your confidence is weak, at least when it comes to your family, the manipulator will work to twist the blame onto you. And this is what I have heard transpire and quite commonly at that.

Hence, this is why I say the concept of forgiveness is a loaded term. The fundamental underpinning of this concept eludes that a certain sequence of steps will release one from the past and permit you to move forward with a happier life. It also alludes to the fact you can do this by yourself and by simply convincing yourself not to hold anger or negative thoughts about the perpetrator. Again, in speaking with many others with PTSD over the years, few ever saw this concept come to fruition. And I believe this is due to the many symptoms of PTSD, which may decline over time, but never go away. The downside of this interaction may also be the fact your intentions are not fully noble, and you subtly may want some form of retaliation. This may be as simple as wanting the other person to feel some level of pain or anguish for how their actions impacted you. Sometimes this may extend further to include some form of physical harm. But as you understand, these thoughts create nothing more than additional memories that you have to deal with later.

The reality is, if you suffer depression or anxiety due to abuse, when such suffering is in a more pronounced state, past memories can come to the forefront. As I mentioned elsewhere, your brain will play tricks on you and it feeds you both real and unreal information. It may be possible for some, but my bad memories from the past have never fully gone away, particularly those involving people. And while the intensity may be significantly less, this is why I feel the concept of forgiveness sounds good on the surface, but in all practicality it doesn't work. My brain can randomly pull those memories back into the forefront even though I don't want it to happen. Hence, that is why I think embracing a near mythical concept is just not realistic. What is a realistic approach is the way and manner you manage your triggers, particularly people.

The concept I do propose for those with PTSD is "forgetting," but not in the sense of completely erasing your memory as it seems just impossible to forget some things. This type of forgetting falls close to the phrase "just forget about it" where releases oneself from the past, and while cognitively the memory remains, emotionally it does not. I saw this point arise in my life after a good amount of counseling where I came to understand what happened to me, how it occurred, what continued to impact me, and how I would manage it going forward. And that defining transition point came when I fully embraced that I was a survivor and not a victim. A survivor mentality acknowledges the events and people of their past, but they choose to move forward from the emotional duress of the past and transition it into positive experiences in the present and for the future. Over time the latter will grow much larger than the past and inherently will make you forget or suppress the negative things of your past.

One element of this approach is to stop being angry about the past and just move forward without it. When you choose to continually dwell on and relive the past, you can find yourself not progressing with your healing. You get stuck per se. This does not mean to ignore the past, but at some point you need to embrace that you are a survivor and no matter how bad your past was, you choose to move forward. And I am saying this from experience as I was stuck for a good period of time on some topics. Part of this was not having the right counseling or support, but also part of this was simply not understanding how to reframe the situations I was in and how to navigate away from the despair and negativity.

Another element of having a survivor mentality--and the most important--is always developing an attitude of being positively focused. Having depression, I fully understand where your mind can take you when you are in a darker place. This of course comes with counseling, but more importantly through practice. The people who you see light up a room and are genuine about it, were not born that way. This was a learned behavior and well-practiced.

It is also tied to gratitude. How you look at your day or events in your life can always be reframed. As an example, a rainy day can either be looked at as a wet, gloomy day or it can be viewed as a great opportunity to catch up on inside tasks. Both end results started with the same factors, yet it is how you reframe them that makes the impact. And it is this approach that used over a long time becomes embedded in your behaviors and redirects you towards positive experience and creating new memories. The more positive memories and actions you can create will only benefit you and ultimately begin to outweigh the wide array of negative memories that can and will hold you back in your life.

THOUGHTS:

GIVING

THOUGHTS ON USING YOUR STRENGTHS TO HELP OTHERS

It was a couple months into a new job and a coworker came to me and suggested I get involved in something to distract my mind. Still being new to the area, I had absolutely no friends, or even acquaintances, and he knew that. He then handed me a newspaper which had an article about a local Methodist Church that had a divorce recovery group. I had not been to church in many years, so I was quite apprehensive and, more so, had no interest in religion or philosophy. I simply wanted direction as to how to stop the hemorrhaging of pain.

By that point, however, I was fully isolating and with the exception of work, had locked myself into my apartment at all other hours except for the bare minimum of interactions, whether it be going to the store for food, the mailbox or the likes of the gas station. Yet at this one moment, something registered and I acquiesced. I knew he was right, but deep down I just didn't feel like doing anything or being with anybody. The world was so ugly to me and wanted nothing to do with it.

As I was barely functioning, I have no recollection of how I actually made myself go to the meeting, when it was or even who was there. The weekly meetings transpired for some time. I still have a copy of the book, *Growing Through Divorce*, that we used in our sessions. I didn't recall the content until recently, but after thumbing through it, the chapters had a myriad of topics that no doubt had to help me. What is interesting is that this recovery program was one of the missions of this church. It had been fully managed and funded by the church, and its impact was significant. I would come to know and trust a number of the people, one of whom many years later would become the godfather of my eldest son.

At the time, I was emotionally needy. Starved is probably more accurate. I needed so much attention and support in all areas to make it to the next day, I felt it was impossible for me to give anything of myself. I felt I was generous in the past, usually with friends, though looking back it is not to the level I would eventually rise too. Was the giving unconditional and from the heart? It probably wasn't. More so, had I ever felt the reciprocation of appreciation? That probably wasn't the case either. My life, as it had been in the military, was very mission-oriented and highly practical. This was all to change and in a way I could have never imagined.

Months after attending this support group, I learned the church had a broad missionary volunteer program. One of the earliest service projects was coordinated at the local Veterans Administration (VA) hospital. I vaguely recall we went there to entertain the residents in the nursing home and have no recollection of whom I was with or what we were doing. By entertain, I mean we were there to give them some companionship. Possibly there were games, music or just conversation. I simply don't recall. But what I do recall is one woman I met by the name of Susie. I am not sure why I sat down with her, but while I was there to cheer her up, something happened that I never could have expected. For some reason I began telling her what had happened to me in recent months. She slowly reached out and held my hand. I can still see and feel her aged skin, which had a somewhat polished look and was cool and smooth to the touch. I don't recall how long I was there, but it must have been about a half hour.

Sitting there crushed and silent, Susie began to talk to me in a comforting way though none of the words registered, with the exception of one sentence. She then profoundly said "Young man, your entire life is still ahead of you." For the first time in many months, this was the very first thing that registered in my mind. Here I was a young man in his early 30s barely surviving, and an elderly woman, coming towards the end or her life, put my life into the proper perspective. I recall when I left the ward I talked to the nurse and shared with her how touched I was by my experience with Susie. The nurse then told me she was 96 and a nurse in World War I. This event is probably the most transformative words of wisdom I have ever received.

As I look back on this, I have little doubt Susie was quite familiar with soldiers with PTSD, though they did not call it such then. She intimately understood what I was experiencing. She understood my manners, expressions, eyes and, of course, my array of emotions. Rightfully, and thankfully, she gave the best advice one can and that is to reframe your situation. You still have your entire life ahead of you. Even though I have struggled many times since, I have never forgotten this wisdom. I do not recall what her face looked like, but I can still see and feel her hand. And that event created a breakthrough moment for me and one element of healing from the past. It would also lead me down a path to over 30 years of volunteer work, some of it significant.

One concept that I would come to embrace is that your struggles can be a blessing. On the surface, it sounds both peculiar and contradictory, particularly if your trauma was extreme. How can a person who has experienced horrible things be grateful for having it happened? Of course, there was much damage and despair, but over time it becomes a smaller percentage of one's life as the good parts increase. And what I discovered was that despite all of the trauma that I had experienced, those same experiences would give me purpose to do some great things.

Life can be simply summarized as often being unfair and quite cruel. And as I often say, "there are only two types of people in this world, those with problems and those that can't admit that they do." Yes, life is unfair to all, though some go through much more difficult events than others. While you are trapped in your despair, you understandably do not recognize that a good portion of people around you are also struggling with their issues. You just never know what they might be going through, as most people are not vocal about their issues publicly. And that is where your experiences become not only powerful, but a blessing. Through your struggles, you have been given the capacity to understand certain issues that only a person with such firsthand experiences would have.

The impact of this first volunteering had such an influence on me that I would participate in many others over the next few years. And while my PTSD symptoms did not seem to be improving, because of the intensity of the many symptoms, they were in fact weakening. I would come to understand later that this time was giving me a brief reprieve from the chaos in my life. While there was the element of being generous, which gives one a positive feeling, this act was providing relief in many other areas.

One benefit of volunteering is that it gave me a break from isolating so extensively in my apartment. Understanding isolation now, this was far more significant than I realized, though I would continue isolating with my behaviors and interaction for many years. Meaning, I was going out in public, but keeping to myself. This effort was low risk and had little anxiety. This was namely walking, or wandering, which I cover in the chapter WALKING, but it was always by myself. Another benefit is that it simply got me moving. If you are suffering depression, you may not want to do much of anything. My depression was a very fluid period with the many symptoms circling around my brain at varying levels of intensity from day to day. I was in a far-away mindset, crippled to inactivity to include even the most basic movements. While I would manage to go to work during the day, I would simply collapse and shelter in place all other hours. This participation was significant and without question helped draw me out of my dark place in the years to come.

Another subtle benefit I experienced was context and perspective. The situations in my life were mostly bad and, in fact, some were very bad. As I participated in a wide array of projects, I would be afforded the opportunity to meet many unique people and hear their stories, often which were filled with tragedy, trauma or simply life challenges. When I listened to them, it gave me a baseline to understand not only how I was doing in the moment, but gave context to my overall life. Some people were better off and struggling with basic things, while others truly were going through some difficult experiences. The one thing about volunteering is that you never know who you will meet. You can start your project feeling great or feeling down, and this can put your life into context.

One project I participated in was a Habitat for Humanity build. I was fairly good with hand tools and thought this would be a way to be creative or in another sense, build something up as so much within my life had been torn down. I vaguely remember the one-story home, but I had another key interaction that further cemented my involvement with volunteering. It was lunch and being a small construction project with a large number of people, there really wasn't anywhere to sit. I saw a man sitting on a makeshift bench, which was basically a piece of plywood laid across a debris pile. I sat down and began to eat my sandwich when he began to talk. I don't recall the exact words, but I do recall the overall content of the conversation. The man, with whom I was talking to, was the recipient of the home we were building. If you aren't familiar with this charity, there is a requirement for the recipient to participate in its construction. He began discussing the struggles of having a place for his family to live and how utterly grateful he was to have this new home. This was more than just a building; it was a home that would grow his family strength. I would think about this moment all day and would come to realize that the value of his new home was about the same as my annual salary. I would also come to realize that as bad as I thought my life was, I did have a place to live in and that I could afford to pay for it. I couldn't have imagined it at the time, this would be a seed to my involvement with similar work in many years ahead. This would eventually evolve to being involved in the building of scores of homes and simpler renovation projects for lower socio-economic families. This no doubt was one of the segues to my future involvement with homeless veterans and women's shelters.

As the years progressed, I stayed with volunteering, the types and amount varied depending on what was going on in life and the time I had available. But I never stopped, and many wonderful experiences transpired. One thing that I came to observe were my many talents and how they could be put to use in volunteering. Each person has unique talents and even the most simple or mundane skills have value in accomplishing broader service. All volunteer organizations or individual efforts need scores of skillsets, ranging from the most very basic tasks to the highest level of leadership and oversight.

As I grew in my profession over the years, I gained numerous skills from my work that would be instrumental in helping me accomplish things in my volunteering. I would come to understand that these were not just talents, but they were really gifts. A talent evolves to a gift, when you have mastered any skill and you subsequently apply it to something you don't expect any compensation for. I am not discounting charitable jobs where one is compensated, but that is not what I am discussing here.

Being that I was an executive in a technical field, I would

groom my communication skills to a very high level, both writing and speaking. As I started my career with an office job, my first responsibility was the launching of very complex products that required the support of cross-functional teams (e.g., engineering, finance, operations, etc.). This required me to listen and communicate with people with inherently different skill sets. It also necessitated me to be able to communicate with fellow employees, customers, consultants and a variety of engineers, all of whom had various levels of technical experience, but who needed a common understanding of the features and benefits of these products. This significantly developed my skill of communicating very complex topics into more simple, understandable concepts and instructions. Professionally, I did very well with this, and it eventually elevated me to an outside position where I worked with top, global clients.

Most of my career was focused on complex products, but after about 10 years, I moved from the industrial to technology sector and found myself in an outside role that combined product management and field engineering. My communication skills became crucial, but they also evolved to where I was developing and designing the products or concepts myself. This was not just due to having technical skills, but also to my experience interfacing with clients who typically had an issue that needed to be resolved. Some of these issues were quite serious and often impacted their broader operations. Over the years, I became quite adept at doing this and feel I made quite a number of significant contributions.

While on the surface it seems as though I am rattling off my resume, what it is in all actuality, is an overview of some of my skills. What I would come to realize, is that these skills would eventually help me accomplish very complicated volunteer projects. I found that I was able to communicate the value of our missions and more importantly, convince people to give their time and money to our cause. If you have ever been involved in fundraising, you know how difficult this is, as people must be convinced of the worthiness of the cause, as well as, you are facing much competition with other charitable causes. I also realized that I was able to interpret and develop initiatives that could accommodate detailed tasks, projects and broader programs. Subsequently over time, I became quite adept at doing this and in my spare time, and in hindsight, the results in terms of donations and accomplishments were somewhat extraordinary. But of course, I could not have foreseen this when I was at my lowest point.

Finding a cause that you can support is not difficult, but it takes some scrutiny. My support of veteran-related PTSD advocacy is where I felt most comfortable, not just emotionally, but how I truly could relate to those people, both veterans and their families, who were suffering from the debilitating symptoms. As you will find, you may have to test several charities or volunteer opportunities before you settle on one. I chose this effort, as I had one small project arise that included a Gold Star mother who had lost her son in the Middle East. I brought my 10-year-old son to a reception, and as I watched her become emotional, I observed how my son went over and comforted her. His simple yet deeply empathetic words, "it will be ok," was a defining moment to make PTSD awareness a lifelong commitment as well as my legacy. In speaking with her later that evening, her comments showed me the impact that could be made, a vision that remains. This also cemented the concept that very small gestures can have a life altering impact.

When selecting a volunteer project or program, I'd like to give some advice. The first and most important, is that volunteer projects include all people, often many of whom are imperfect. Inherently, volunteer work is an effort of imperfect people working to do perfect things. The second is anxiety, and it is present in all organizations. When you go into something new, you need to temper your expectations and understand that you will be working with imperfect people who may do and say things that either annoy or trigger you. As well, and as you probably know, people can react in such a way that it can cause you overall anxiety. It is your responsibility to control how you react and subsequently manage through this. Personally, I have left a couple efforts as I saw a broader, underlying issue that I did not think met my overall objectives or where I would feel uncomfortable. I ultimately ended up leaving them, but I did so quietly and without anger.

For myself, I had enough positive experiences with PTSD advocacy, that I wanted to continue with expanding my contribution to this mental health issue. And in part, this is how this book was written. I did not have an intention to write this book, but after enough time discussing how I moved forward with my illness, I saw that my diary notes and my writing skills of complex topics lent itself to one. Hopefully, the thoughts here are registering with you and will help fill in some of the holes of your journey.

My symptoms at times subside, but one or more are usually present. I think because of the familiarity with our symptoms, it is human nature to want to align to those causes that align with our own. I most certainly did and that was due to a number of factors. But I caution you that there are a number of reasons why you should involve yourself to other projects that are outside of this.

Besides the reciprocation of appreciation, possibly one of the most tangible benefits is the rebuilding of trust. Without question, the issue of trusting people is the most frequent topic I hear discussed by those with PTSD. Most certainly it remains at the top of my list and why I wrote the chapter TRUSTING. No matter what volunteer project you select, it is imperative that you choose one that will not drive your anxiety. And that can be a very fine line, particularly if you choose to volunteer in a service that supports those who have been traumatized. The very people you help, may have symptoms similar to yours, and you must be careful not to absorb their issues. This falls under the same concept of don't bring your work home with you.

It has been my observation that the lower the anxiety there is in a project, the lower risk of it triggering your responses. I have personally experienced that arts-based volunteering may be the best as you can lower your defenses and be more relaxed. If you find you are still hyper-vigilant, start with small, short-term tasks. But to say it again, people can still act up. Generally, the people who are doing artistic or creative things are doing these activities to escape the chaos of the world and just want to have fun. For myself, I have always been fairly artistic. While I had done much wood working from a young age, I would find myself building theater sets for a period of time and later structures for museum dioramas and model railroads. I would also find myself painting a variety of things over the years.

It is in these settings that you will meet caring and gentle people who will accept you for who you are. More so, these people will appreciate your time and talents, even though it may be difficult for you to accept their appreciation. I personally found myself being fulfilled beyond my expectations. And to this, I have no doubt that when I was unconditionally helping with the right intentions, I was rewarded with unconditional respect and, at times, love.

All of these experiences in totality will build trust with another person and subsequently connect you to the outside world. It will also give you the opportunity to express yourself in a positive way when so much in your life may seem negative. It will sooth your soul and bring balance. The very best thing is that you can volunteer now, even as you set this chapter down. And while I have a number of technical skills, it does not matter what skill you have and the fact it can be useful in helping others. Nearly anything that you are capable of doing has value to others. And it is this that will help break isolation and begin building trust in others. Looking back all this time, I could have never foreseen that the one act of going to a nursing facility and being kind to another human being would significantly transform the rest of my life.

THOUGHTS:

HELPING

THOUGHTS ON FINDING VARIOUS TYPES OF SUPPORT

It goes without saying, but you will need support and possibly quite a bit. Depending on which PTSD symptoms you have, you will not only need different professionals, but also friends and family, as well as support groups. And not to be pushy, but this is not an option. You may believe you are ok or you may believe you will be fine or you may believe you are able to do this on your own. I have been in all three places and when even by the most logical rationalizations created in my mind, it still was not rational looking back upon it. I don't recall who told me this expression, but it was a very long time ago and I have used it often. They said, "if you don't ask for help, don't expect it." But that said, I am here to tell you, even when you ask for it, you still may not get it or actually what you need. You may also need to ask for it more than once and from multiple sources.

Firstly, the beginning part of this chapter is slanted towards veterans only for the fact that if you are not within the Veterans Administration (VA) system, you will approach your medical help like all others. Though if you are filing for Social Security Disability, you will see some parallels. While much of this is relevant for all, I have offered some thoughts about getting help as a Veteran, as certain types of help require different strategies and tactics. As well, the following is an overly simplified version, but it will allow you to generally understand where you can get assistance. And to that, I am going to give some frank observations. These of course are my observations and yours may vary. But treat it like a data point.

If you are a veteran, you will be in one of four stages of getting help. The first stage is what I have termed Pre-VA. This is where you believe you have PTSD stemming from your military service and have the intent to file for some level of disability. This can be confusing and quite overwhelming, but there are better approaches than others. And by approaches I really mean strategies and tactics. Strategies are your game plans and tactics are the specific things you do.

When I applied for disability my first time, I did it myself by using the respective VA form. In my submission I had the proof I needed that showed the incidents that both created and exacerbated my PTSD. Remember, you are going to have to have evidence. This can in part come from your DD214, but in my case, it did not have all the information I thought it should have. And having talked with others who depended on their DD214, their records also did not fully show what duty they went through. I'm not sure if this is due to security reasons or lack of detail and effort. If there is inadequate detail, this may require you to have at least a witness or documentation of some sort. I was fortunate that there was an official family newsletter that described not only what happened, but mentioned my name. I will note that recordkeeping appears to be better now than when I served, but do not be surprised. I can tell you that in my further research of the general service we did, that too was annotated quite vaguely, but believe in part that was due to part of our missions.

While I filled out the form myself, and while I am fairly well educated and articulate, it was not easy. My advice is to approach a

Veterans organization, of which there are many, and utilize their free services. I've known people to hire a specialized attorney, but they will take a pretty good chunk of your money for payment. If you feel comfortable filling it out, remember you are going to need to follow up with it. The only downside to using one of these services is the reality that they can be quite overwhelmed helping many Veterans. You will have to be patient, possibly follow up regularly, and be prepared to look at an additional source of support if you don't make progress.

The second stage is what I have termed Post-VA application. This is the period that you have submitted the claim form and begun the process to be reviewed. This also includes that the VA has acknowledged your claim and begins the process of interviewing you and subsequently sending the findings to their board for review. If you have multiple issues, the VA will send you to multiple interviews. My advice here is the same as applying for any entry level job. Get your foot in the door. Meaning, your goal is to get at least a part of your claim acknowledged so you get into the system. I will go into this further later.

My first interview surprised me in both the intensity and speed. I don't know if this was purposeful, but I always wondered if they were trying to trip me up in my answers. This first interview was done by a VA employee who pushed me very hard and asked a number of the same questions in different ways. The interview also seemed to be timed. They asked the questions quickly, regularly prompting me to go faster. The best advice I will give you is practice repeatedly so you can clearly and quickly explain your story to the interviewer. By practicing, you will not only project being more confident, but that will come across as truthful. It will also help the interviewer be more articulate in their notes. If you fumble around with your answers, you may not get the expected results, even if you are telling the truth.

In some of my future claim interviews, the VA contracted third party doctors to complete them. From what I have gathered they are not paid very well to do this, and while they may be more compassionate, you should still be prepared to talk quickly. One thing I have also done is take my VA information, as in doctor's names, appointments and decisions, to discuss at the meeting. I feel this helped them gather thoughts and wording for their reports. I did have one bad experience with one of these doctors, but then appealed to see another doctor. Remember, you have more flexibility in your claim process than you think you do. I will say though, if the VA is backlogged, which it was on my claims, it could take months to get a response.

Now from a more human perspective, I found the interview to be very difficult emotionally. While I knew the detail intimately, as it had been running through my head for two decades, the intensity and the types of questions caused a good amount of anxiety to me. I vividly remember shaking for the latter part of the interview and by the end, I was completely numb. I subsequently had an extended panic attack and cried. My advice is that you have a support person go with you to the visit, having the full knowledge of talking you down if you are overwhelmed. In fact, I have often done this at future doctor visits of all types. I have found that because of my PTSD, my fight and flight responses are elevated and can start diminishing my current thoughts. That support person can keep you calm and as well, feed you details you should discuss. Another reason to do this is that the interviewer may not have resources for you should you go into an anxiety or panic attack. On my first interview for the VA, I was so mentally drained that I was physically unable to drive home. Make note of this.

The third stage is being VA Processed. You will get a notice in the mail confirming or not confirming your disability. I can tell you that the results can be illogical, but as mentioned earlier, your goal is to get your foot in the door. Most veterans who have been in the system for a while understand that to increase your benefits, you will most likely need to apply again. Though the facts of what got me my first rating never changed, what did change were the symptoms as they worsened. I personally went from 30%, to 50% and then finally to 70% PTSD rating. In my opinion, when I was classified as 50%, I really was 70%, but it required perseverance.

As a side note, this is really important and may confuse you during the process. The VA looks at your mental health as one classification, while your doctor at the VA hospital may discuss multiple illnesses, the VA board appears to group them together as one. In my case, my general anxiety disorder became quite severe over time and created new symptoms. When I filed for that separately, the administrative side (aka who reviews the cases) grouped it as part of my PTSD. This is one of those cases that did not seem logical to me because it was creating its own issues. As it was explained to me, and which could change, is that all mental health issues are grouped together in one rating. If you have multiple issues, I would work to define your issues and symptoms as accurate as possible before you file, so when you submit your claim, it annotates the totality. This is not necessarily easy and as I mentioned, my symptoms evolved over time.

When you file for PTSD, you should also fully understand all of the respective percentages, which reflect the severity and impact to your life. For me, my PTSD was finally rated at 70%, and by definition, my symptoms were 'nearly constant' and impacting most facets of my life. When you read the definitions of each, think about how to discuss your symptoms so they best match the rating you see yourself in. My symptoms were in fact nearly constant and had permeated every layer of my life. This is the list I prepared, which I took to my interview. This of course does not guarantee you that actual rating, as it may come in lower or higher, but it gives you both a strategy and language to discuss how you see yourself. The interviewer will also be asking you a wide range of questions, which will also help them identify the severity. It is also prudent to list your symptoms on paper when you go to any doctor, whether in the VA or any other healthcare provider.

What do you do if the VA denies your claim? This is probably somewhat relevant for a Social Security claim as well. There could be a number of reasons why this happens, but realize the process is still not over. Firstly, knowing a number of veterans in the system, I have heard some of the most obvious issues be ignored. I've known veterans to have nearly identical issues, yet one is approved and the other isn't. You may get quite frustrated, most certainly when the decision is illogical considering the facts. I have often wondered who the reviewers were and what their capability was. I also wondered if it could be as simple as the reviewer had a bad day.

A second reason your claim could have been denied, and as noted earlier, there may have been inadequate information of some sort. Hence, why I said preparing is crucial. If you are able to gather new or additional information, you can simply resubmit the claim. An alternate approach is appealing the decision. If you weren't aware, the VA has different forms for these approaches.

In one of my claims, I swore they never even read my existing and current VA medical records. In a response to my claim, they said something that literally contradicted the facts that were extensive in my medical records. And it was no small service-related issue. This really showed the disconnect between the medical and administrative sides with the VA. Again, do as much as you can to help them help you.

If you filed your claim by yourself, this is the time I recommend that you engage with a veteran's organization. As I have multiple issues in my disability, I had a follow-up visit that wiped out part of one of my ratings. I subsequently went to an organization to assist, and they filed the appeal. While I felt this change was actually due to incompetence, it was after this assistance that the VA came back and acknowledged they made a partial error. I'm aware that is quite a rare occurrence. But the fact is, it gave me more support. In this case, I appealed and succeeded.

There is some wisdom I would like to impart regarding your VA experience. No matter what illogical or inadequate decision is made, and while you have the right to be frustrated, you must keep your cool. That is with any person within the VA or outside organization helping you. Remember, they are people, who are not only infallible, but who behave like the broader population. Your task here is like a job interview. You are trying to get a job. Whether you like them or not, or what they have to say, be nice at all times. I have known a couple of people who felt their verbal responses and behaviors led to the person they were engaged with to retaliate.

Let's discuss other types of support that may be helpful, if not crucial:

988

While there are crisis hotlines, this one is the simplest to use on your phone. If you are at that point of being so overwhelmed and are giving up hope, pick up the phone. While I don't know this to be a fact, my guess is most of the people on the other side of the phone have been where you are. The number of people who have walked your walk is significant and they can help you get grounded and validate your feelings. I have been here and implore you to call. I also recommend putting this in in your cell phone contacts.

FRIENDS AND FAMILY

During my breakdown, I had two friends and a sister who were my first line of defense. While they can typically give you the most sincere and empathetic support, I feel that window may be a small one. Keep in mind that while they care for you, they are most likely not trained professionals. In the simplest of terms, you don't call an electrician to fix a leaking pipe. I use that term, because trained professionals know how to begin to turn off supply valves. They not only have both the vocabulary and skills, they also have access to resources. Certainly, my situation was so serious that I have little doubt I wore my friends out. I think they were polite at first, but that support ended somewhat quickly. Another issue that really made this harder was the fact was my closest friend was 100 miles away and my sister was hundreds of miles away. You need someone local.

PSYCHOLOGIST

Their primary role, like other licensed counselors, is to observe and interpret your emotional state and behavior. They may offer the best resources for helping you understand where your mental health is on a number of spectrums. It surprises some when I say this, but they work for you. You need to pick one that is suited to understand PTSD. In my case, not one of my pre-VA doctors ever diagnosed me with PTSD, but they did diagnose me with depression. Depending on your trauma type, they should be able to tell you their experience, and more so, whether they specialize in it.

There are some personal experiences I would like to share here. If you get a provider that you don't connect with or if you think they aren't helping you, go get another. Do not continue with them because as time passes and you don't improve, you may give up on using one altogether. I personally had a couple of weak providers and it surfaced by their lack of organization and preparation as well as the low caliber of the questions they asked. You do not want them to ask easy questions, because it won't pull out all of the issues impairing your recovery. If you are in the VA system, and if you have plans on expanding your claims, they will become an advocate for you as they will put your health data into the main system. If you don't have any appointments, you may project you might not be as severe as you think you are.

One issue which is plaguing much of the medical world, particularly mental health, is wait times. If you cannot get an appointment in a timely manner, I would recommend calling your PCP and see if they can assist. If you are in a more complex situation and feel at risk, no matter how small of an amount, I would go to Urgent Care, who might be able to facilitate quicker assistance for you.

PSYCHIATRIST

This is usually a doctor (M.D.), but within the VA I have also had a nurse practitioner. The role of the psychiatrist is to prescribe medications that address your symptoms. As a warning up front, this was a longer journey for me. The field is not a perfect science and requires them to test medications from different groups, try combinations of them as well as adjust dosages. Over time, I did not respond well to a number of medications, and, in fact, found I was allergic to one group. But the process can take weeks or even months for there to be a noticeable change. This does require some patience.

One thing I would like to make note of is some people go to their primary care physician for medication. My observation, and remember this is mine, mental health is not their primary job and why a psychiatrist is so very important. Remember, today's psychiatrists go through significant education that continues throughout their entire career. They are most adept to understanding the complexity of medications, and they are aware of new studies and medications on this topic.

PRIMARY CARE PHYSICIAN (PCP)

It is important to let your PCP be aware of what is going on. Interestingly, it was my PCP who first diagnosed me with a Generalized Anxiety Disorder, which I thought was the symptoms of another illness. But besides their obvious role, they can do an array of testing to gauge how your whole body is sustaining. They can also give you guidance for other help, as well. If you are within the VA, the three specialists will be able to read each other's notes. This is also the benefit of being within a larger medical health care provider as they too can see all of your notes. They are your care team and you may find it helpful to check in with them to let them know what is going on. The key word here is "team" and it will often take one.

GROUP THERAPY

It goes without saying, if you are fighting an addiction, that one of the most powerful resources is Alcoholics Anonymous (AA) or Narcotics Anonymous (NA). If you think there is a stigma to attending, I assure you there are a vast array of people, from all aspects of life, that attend these meetings. While I fortunately never faced this, I have attended many meetings and heard messages that equaled some of the best life lessons I've heard from motivational speakers.

The second type of group therapy are those that are trauma specific. I say this as different trauma events cause PTSD. If you are a woman, you may want to be in an all-women's group. If you are a veteran, you most likely want to be in an all-veteran's group. I have attended the latter and can tell you it has helped to frame my thoughts, reflect on other's experiences, given me skills to think about and simply provided human interaction with people who really understand you. It was within one of these groups that I first was able to speak about the darkest topics a veteran may have experienced. These groups, though not always, are supported by non-profits, veteran organizations and sometimes churches. If you are really feeling burdened, group therapy may be one of the best and quickest tools at your disposal. They can typically be found on Craigslist, Facebook, internet queries or the back of newspapers. Your licensed professionals helping you many also be aware of possible groups.

EMPLOYER HR

If it makes sense and you work for a solid employer, talk to your HR person. When I broke down, I did not have this option, and there were not legal protections that there are today. While I believe I was able to work, my guess is that I was acting out in various degrees. If you need time off for appointments, or if you need to take a leave of absence to get additional care, this is the only way to safeguard your job. The law does not require you to tell your boss, nor can they ask, but this information shared with HR can provide some protection for your employment and more so, they too may have resources to help you.

ONLINE SOURCES

As much of the world is moving to streamed content online, so has the information for understanding PTSD. While this content does not replace the value and purpose of licensed professionals or a support group, it can greatly improve your knowledge, much like a book does. The online content appears to fall into a number of groups and I will go through those. The first is websites that are generally hosted by professionals or organizations. These sites often give high-level information, but appear to be developed to draw you into using their purchased services. So when you read them, just be aware of this.

The second is social media, with Facebook appearing to be the leading source. You will note that there are several PTSD pages with some having slightly different focuses from one another. As these don't always appear to be run by professionals, you need to temper your expectations. Possibly the greatest value you can find from such sources is the broad explanation of concepts, new terminology and maybe most importantly, the validation of what you are feeling. You may be surprised how many people are on these pages, which can put context to your situation that you are not alone, and as well, simply have a fellow human being acknowledge your personal thoughts. There are some cautions however and you need to be prepared for them. The first is that people can be imperfect in their actions and responses, as they too may be experiencing duress from trauma. These people's words and behaviors can possibly offend you and more so be a trigger. The second are inappropriate posts, that include the promotion of remedies or therapists trying to poach patients for their online services. Sadly, I have seen this quite a few times. This is not only unethical , but it usually violates the page's rules. If you see this, report them to the group administrator to address.

The third source of information I will group together is Youtube and Podcasts. Often these are facilitated by professionals or hosts that interview professionals. Personally, I have been quite amazed by the quality of content as well as how concise and articulate it is. Possibly the greatest value is that they are readily available 24/7 and you can watch any time of the day and multiple times. I personally have watched some content multiple times to better reinforce a concept. Some of my breakthroughs have in fact come from these sources and with this information, I have taken notes and further discussed it with my counselor or psychiatrist.

WRITING

Granted this is a self-help book, but it was created by me journaling for years. I journaled all the time and about all topics. Some of it was useful; some of it was rambling. But if you are drowning in thoughts, put them down on paper. I often left space and subsequently wrote more about that topic later. I cannot emphasize how important this approach is as I would use it to document literally every aspect of my life. I think the most obvious is that it can help you download the information in your head and put it on paper. I discuss this in the chapter RESTING.

There are other approaches, which I may address in a later revision. However, I cannot emphasize enough how very important it is for you to prepare for your own healing. The very best licensed professionals will only be able to help you so much as the time of your interaction will be limited. You simply may not get as much professional support as you desire or that they are able to allocate with you. Hence your work between meetings is crucial and this will let you be better prepared so you can use their time wisely, and continue your healing effectively.

THOUGHTS:

ISOLATING

THOUGHTS ON BEING LONELY AND ALONE

Despite the chaos in my childhood, I generally did not isolate myself from others. At first, I thought about naming this chapter AVOIDING, because isolation is part of a much broader avoidance strategy.

As I discuss in the chapter CUTTING, I put much distance between my parents and myself in my adulthood, but I actually started doing this as a child by staying fairly busy. In fact, I recall enjoying being by myself as a kid, but not in the sense of isolating. Children with different types and intensities of trauma embrace different strategies, but as early as five I was smart enough to recognize that it was best not to be near my parents. Of course, this strategy really was not a strategy as much as it was a consequence of not wanting to be around them. I simply kept away from them and discovered that by spending time with friends, I established the distance I desired (or needed) and also some level of normalcy.

From the age of 5 to 11, I was probably gone from my house two thirds of the day and did this by going to school early and was involved with friends and functions that would lead into the late afternoon. Activities throughout my youth like church youth group, theater, soccer and band filled the greatest void, as they were not only a creative outlet but gave me the companionship and nurturing that I was not getting at home. By the time I was eleven, I was quite ambitious and started doing yard work after school and on the weekends. This allowed me to make fairly good money for being a kid, as it funded about anything I wanted to do away from home.

Childhood trauma can cause both shame and embarrassment and to some degree I felt the latter. This was not prevalent, though I was embarrassed to bring friends around not knowing how my parents might act. My father put on a good show outside of the home, and with a strong and deep bass voice he made his presence known. It has been strange in my adulthood to hear positive comments about him, making me believe he hid his true behaviors fairly well in public, and for those who I knew closely, I did a pretty good job of hiding his behaviors by keeping them away from him.

Kids before the 1980s had a lot more freedom than they do today. Anyone who understands the concept that you went home when the streetlights turned on, recognizes we had the freedom to play and explore until dark. It was a different time and parents, whether correct or not, didn't worry about their kids being away from the house. Bicycles were ridden by all and the pile of them in front of a house or park gave the update most parents were looking for. But the fact is, I was gone far more than that, often long after the streetlights came on, and don't ever recall my parents being concerned. Possibly my parents asked what I was doing, but don't recall that I ever got in trouble for being out too late. My guess is the busy schedule of activities put on a front that I was in good hands. However, I wasn't always doing those activities as I became a teenager. I was doing other things.

Not being able to get into their thoughts, I've always wondered whether they even cared or more so, knew that they should have. I observed my friends' relationships with their parents and was admittedly envious. What I saw in their relationships was completely void in mine. In all the attributes of being a good parent, my parents fell short. Hence, I spent a great deal of time with friends and wondered if their parents knew what was going on in my home. They may have or may have not known. I know that our relatives knew, though it would be well into my adulthood that I learned of their ambivalence and selfishness, as they did nothing. I don't believe my parents were malevolent, as much as they were just clueless and their own personal mental health issues dwarfed their responsibilities and dominated their behaviors.

By the age of 16 I was already engaging with military recruiters and at 17 joined the Navy. It was the post-Vietnam-War era, and the world was relatively quiet. In fact, I don't remember much about Vietnam until it was ending. This may have been due to the fact I wasn't home when the news might have been on, but I don't recall it ever being part of my everyday life to include school. I recall fringe events, such as the peace movement, but never recall even seeing anyone in a uniform. There absolutely was never a protest. So going into the Navy felt relatively safe. It not only put more distance and time between me and my parents, but was also a path forward to some type of job and life in the future. My parents coincidentally had made absolutely no preparation for me post high school, but this was a consistent pattern for their entire life.

The first major movement into isolation was about my second year in the Navy when I was deployed to the Middle East. This level of trauma is nearly indescribable as it was very complex. I was in a mission critical command that was obliged to front line service, which truly had me scared for the first time in my life. We were not only in harm's way, but it was for extended periods of time. This was magnified by the fact that we not only had what I thought was poor leadership, but the workdays were grueling with watch (guard duty) being 8 or 12 hours a day on top of long, working hours. Anyone who has worked shift duty intimately understands this.

And while I believe enlisted personnel have far more rights today, what we were going through could be categorized as both mentally and physically abusive. I'm not saying it was all targeted, though some was at times, but it was just how the grind of the duty transpired in some military duty of the time. I attribute this now in part that the leadership's formative years was during Vietnam.

Because we were deployed in theater for so long and having to work long days from 16 to 20 hours, the free time was very fragmented. As your watch rotated, this made it far more complex as your body never really regulated to a schedule. When you were off, you may have only had a break for a few hours, but this time was often comprised of eating, sleeping and in the worst scenario, drills or general quarters. It was hence the combination of situational factors of violence, duress, and little personal space coupled with exhaustion and weak emotional, management skills that embedded isolation into my behavior. I remember at the worst times how I would retreat into myself and attempt to turn off the world around me. It didn't work well, and this left me deeply dispirited and sometimes nearly despondent. Time habitually dragged as the measurement of time changed. Days were reduced to hours and sometimes minutes depending on how much chaos there was. Each hour seemed like an eternity, and after two plus years of this, it took an absolute toll on my mental health.

While I may have felt I was improving after this duty, I have come to understand many years later that I was only masking it. This formative period established isolation as one of my key coping mechanisms. I may have not shown it outwardly to others, but it was ever present and had a very strong grip on every aspect of my thinking. The need to protect myself from being harmed was heightened and can only in hindsight, reflect as to how hard I was avoiding certain things in my life. And from here it evolved past just being with people, as in not wanting to be with or around people; it also developed into a parallel avoidance to places and things as well. Outwardly I continued forward, but inwardly I was contracting.

After the military I went to college and was a fairly good student. I retained the discipline that I had learned in the military, which led to a very busy schedule of classes, work and studies. While it was a more mundane environment than being in the military, there was still an exhaustive intensity and fatigue. Looking back at this period as well, I was so busy that I had little time for much of anything else. Though I had interaction with others, it was somewhat superficial, namely due to need, and they seemingly posed little risk. I did have a couple close friends, but the time with them was usually compressed. Again, being so busy I was mentally in a fairly safe place, and my PTSD symptoms suppressed. Clearly, I had been ignoring the trauma I had been through, which subsequently created additional layers of avoidance.

Fast forward several years, my failed marriage made me emotionally vulnerable, unraveling and magnifying numerous negative coping skills to the point where they became permanently ingrained. All of my past came rushing out and I mentally broke down. I was living in a relatively new city and had just started a new job. There literally was no one to turn to, no one to help me and more so, no one to hold me. I was in deep emotional trouble and that lack of immediate support exacerbated a situation of feeling both abandoned and stranded. I literally did not know what to do or where to go and that absolutely aided my free fall. And hence a situation arose where many different events, including mundane ones not related to my past traumas, were now triggering negative thoughts and behaviors. What healing that may have occurred since my separation from military service, returned with a vengeance. All of my thoughts evolved to a place quite similar to that dark period of time. My negative thoughts were unbridled, and intense flashbacks occurred at all hours of the day.

For the first time in my life I was truly lonely, and the negative thoughts in my head had now drowned out most every other thought, particularly any positive ones. This negative state moved far beyond people and the trust of them, but it became an issue about myself and living in a dark world by myself. I began isolating my real life, and despite the fact that some things were actually going ok, I fell into a world consumed by negative distortion and believing that everything was going wrong. I was also isolating myself from myself, and the small world that I was in continued to grow smaller and the mental challenges more complex. The problem arose that my thought processes had been reversed to the point it created an exaggerated avoidance strategy.

It is difficult to measure loneliness. While I had felt lonely in the military, I was not alone and was going through that trauma with others. Yet this time, the emotions were so overwhelming and debilitating that I didn't know what to do with them. The combination of profound feelings of rejection and abandonment, fatigue from the many recent life changes, and the brewing symptoms of the PTSD created an untenable cocktail of despair. Because I had no support network, this greatly compounded the problems and transformed these emotions into a much broader state of being alone. What I experienced was to such a degree and complexity that it registered at the highest level just before committing suicide. I was crushed.

In later years as I tried to understand what happened, all I had were the random notes in my diary. My memory had already suppressed much detail, and because of my severe mental health decline, much of what transpired around me just never registered. What information I had on my state of health gave only a high-level snapshot of my behaviors, which were typically the symptoms causing me the most pain. This information, of course, was also written through the eyes of an ill person, which was an obscured view, if not a partial cognitive distortion of reality. Meaning, the writings were a blending of truth and philosophy verses being an accurate assessment or diagnosis of what was going through my head. In even simpler words, it was organized rambling from a disorganized mind.

The reason I went into length on my past is that these coping mechanisms are far more complex than just isolation. They are about being lonely and alone. There are some similarities between them, but they are not the same and the driving forces that push you to one of them are different. Understanding why and when these took a foothold in your life is important, if you want to escape being stuck with your past experiences. Isolation is not just a state, but an ever-changing strategy of avoidance, and it requires one to recognize what triggers one to want to be alone. For myself, the complex symptoms of PTSD created many triggers, some less rational than others. These subsequently created patterns of behaviors and reactions that continued to break down connections with people, or conversely, prevented them from occurring.

I gained some wisdom as to what I wish I understood when I was at the bottom and would like to share that with you. Because cognitive distortion was on full throttle and I was well into suicidal ideation, I clearly needed support for nearly every aspect of my life. I go into length as to how I did this in the chapter LEARNING, but it is paramount to talk with someone whether it be a counselor or a support group. You will have to create some method to be able to rationalize and congeal your thoughts, and at a minimum, to try to harness and tame the negative thoughts outweighing those things that might actually be going well.

Life is going to continue and as we are inherently social creatures, we are obliged to interact with other people. Admittedly, I moved to a place where I generally hated all people and trusted absolutely nobody. While some of this was warranted, it evolved to a degree where I recognized it went too far, though I did not know how to undo it. There also remained the feeling that I necessarily didn't want it to change. Over many years in speaking with people who were former military, particularly those with bad duty, this is often spoken of. No matter what life or trauma experiences you went through, finding a support group will put you on parity with others.

There will be some relationships such as family, particularly kids, and work you will have to be present for. And it is for these responsibilities that your healing or management of them will at a minimum need to occur. In my case, I didn't have children yet, but now understand the intensity of their care can distract you from caring for yourself. Regarding work, I recall performing well enough, but was inwardly focused for the most part and acted out my responsibilities accordingly. I may have come across as normal to others, though without question some of my behavior was off. Somehow, I conducted myself in a way to get my work done, but now understanding how sick I was, I remain absolutely amazed as to how I actually pulled it off. Did I really care about the people around me or develop stronger friendships or relationships? I don't think I did and this may or may not have shown. I was of course in a survival mode. In hindsight, I wish I had the opportunity to leave the area and get support from someone. But that someone did not exist.

When off from work, I would often walk a great deal which gave me time to reflect about myself and my life. I discuss this in length in the chapter WALKING, which gave me a sense of peace, but more so, it simply removed a number of the negative stimulations. At times I would go to the mountains, and this would be the first place that I would find absolute solitude. The peace and comfort I found there would become the first positive skills I would learn regarding self-soothing. This kept me alone and created a feeling of safety that I embraced. I came to a place where I was comfortable being alone and doing a variety of things by myself. Hence, I limited my interactions with people to ones only out of necessity, and my social connections were eliminated. While self-soothing is important, the degree I took this isolation was probably too far, though at the same time, it was probably the healthiest approach I could have taken considering all of the PTSD symptoms that I was experiencing.

At this point, my choice to be alone was not the best approach, but as I didn't have support or counseling services, it provided the safest place for me to recover. I recognize there is a fairly fine line between being alone and being antisocial. I no doubt fluctuated between the two. My guess is I stayed in this elevated state for a few years, when it began to morph into a different state where I came to enjoy being alone. This was more than just being safe, but more the fact that I felt at rest and could let my guard down and relax.

Since this time, it has taken a tremendous amount of work to become more social. In fact, the intensity of my breakdown laid the groundwork for isolation that would last to varying degrees for decades. Depending on what caused your trauma, to include its intensity and impact, you will mostly likely be triggered by people, places and things in the future. As I like to explain it, I was taken past a point where the rubber band just did not go back to its original shape.

Fortunately, I made wise decisions selecting my second wife and we have been together nearly three decades. We are best friends, and I really enjoy spending time with her, even if it is doing my own thing in proximity to her. Likewise, I have very strong relationships with my kids. Is a relationship with your partner or kids enough? There may not be a straightforward answer, but for your own well-being and personal growth it probably isn't.

Being willing to expose yourself and connecting with new people is awkward at best. Finding balance with loneliness, being alone and avoidance is going to take practice. In the chapter TRUSTING, I discuss my approaches, but it comes down to being rationally smarter and methodical. I have continued to struggle making new friends. Admittedly, my expectations are high, possibly too high at times. This will come down to what type of friend you are looking for and how much risk you are willing to expose yourself too. If you are looking for casual friendship, both the risk and expectations are lower. If you are looking for a close friendship, this may take a more methodical approach. I believe it doesn't just happen. It takes some thought, preparation and planning.

I have made connections with people, though the results of some evolved differently than I thought they would have, and have subsequently learned a couple approaches. Firstly, if you are former military, you will inherently bond quicker to those from the same pool of experiences. Likewise, you may bond quicker to someone who is also healing from mental health issues. While there are many shared commonalities with these types of people, I encourage you to go past them and look at activities where there is a potential for little anxiety. Interests such as volunteer work, creative outlets like art or music, or outdoor activities will pair you with people just wanting to be good people. This is not to say there won't be difficult people, but more likely than not, it will be people trying to do good for others and it gives a venue for you to be potentially happy in a lower-risk environment. Possibly the greatest advantage is that they are much less likely to talk about things that trigger you and remind you of your past.

Does the desire to isolate ever get better? I don't believe there is an easy answer to this, but lean towards the fact it may, though it may never be the same as before your trauma. As you understand, once trust has been broken to a certain degree or a significant trauma has occurred, it rewires your brain and the way you interpret situations and subsequently react. Life continues forward, and it and the people around you, are imperfect and unfair. What does change, however, is how you choose to respond to it. To this, the causes that attempt to drive your thought processes won't change, but your reactions and their impact to your mental health will. The ability to increase your tolerance and decrease your wanting to isolate will take much practice.

To be fully transparent, I have continued to struggle with trust and relationships. This has improved, though admittedly not to where I thought it would. People want to read or hear solutions as to how they can heal. This is compounded because people who are out to make money in the healing process will lead you to believe it may be easy as a multi-step process. Meaning, if you do this and you do that, you will move forward, creating new relationships and a happier life. While this may be possible for some, this just has not come easy for me at any level, and for those I know with PTSD, it does not come easy for them either. It will simply come down to finding people who build you up and pull you away from your past and subsequently, you will want to spend more time with them verses wanting to be alone.

THOUGHTS:

LEARNING

THOUGHTS ON COUNSELORS AND COUNSELING

Mental health is a strange science for the average person. Each of us has experiences, both good and bad, that we build upon our entire life. How we process and manage them is a lifelong challenge as we circumnavigate the complexities of our understandings, behaviors, and management of them. But the mental health profession has its own terms and knowledge base it doesn't typically share with patients to depth that I think they should. Meaning mental health professionals do not go into the nuts and bolts of your issues. They might not give you the technical names of the symptoms or they won't go into depth on what the symptoms are doing to you physically. In the simplest of terms, they may dumb it down and give generalized input.

The fact is nobody knows you better than you do. Depending on where you are with your recovery, some of what I say may resonate and some may seem critical. Also, some of this parallels the chapter HELPING, but this goes beyond the sources and sets some goals you should set with not only yourself, but with them. The following is not only my personal observations, but also input from a wide variety of people I have met and sources that I have read or heard. And when I say criticism, I also mean this more from a constructive criticism that can help expedite your experiences and growth. If you have the expectation that the VA or a counselor outside of that system is going to do the heavy lifting, that is simply not going to happen. What you can find is that you are a "number" in a big bureaucracy and "minutes" in a small one. And if you have ever heard or experienced that the system or counselor was not as useful as was hoped, much of that burden remains on the patient, but not completely. You are going to have to learn new things, particularly the more technical aspects of your issues, and subsequently become a project manager of your wellbeing. The more you know technically about yourself, the better questions and strategies you will be able to develop to move forward. The other half of learning is making sure your counselor is also helping you learn, and that requires more finesse.

When I entered the VA system, I had the belief they would manage me as a person and help me improve the wide array of issues I was facing. After years of counseling and having a variety of counselors with different certifications and experiences, I saw a reappearing pattern where I felt that I was missing some type of detail or understanding of what was really going on with me. I often found that I was asking them more thought-provoking questions as to what was going on with me than vice versus. What I discovered was that I had to personally learn more about mental health symptoms outside the care of the system, so I could push the system to help me. In fact, this is where my greatest gains came from with moving forward.

There is practicality to this approach and it is a term that I have coined "mindshare." The traditional definition is a marketing term, but have altered it to mean how much time that you are sharing your mind. This is very important and will put the rest of this chapter into perspective. When I was at my worst, I really was obsessing on negative thoughts a significant portion of each day, but it was most prevalent during my time outside of work. Let's say your negative thoughts are top of mind for four hours a day, which equals about 120 hours in a month. If you are only seeing a therapist twice a month for 50 minutes sessions, where you are only actively working on your issues, that is less than two percent of your negative thoughts. That's not very much and you can play with the numbers to match your reality. And this is why doing much of the footwork yourself is imperative and why you will hear those, who are well into their healing say "it takes a lot of work." It in fact takes a great deal of work and you have to create all types of positive content to outweigh the negative content.

This also tempered my understanding of the care I was or wasn't getting as well as the strategy I needed to embrace going forward. It also meant I was going to be ultimately in charge of my mental health care and progress. Meaning you are going to have to learn and teach yourself so you can advocate for the best care. This isn't such a strange concept if you had a serious illness such as cancer, or even a more common illness such as diabetes. It is common that you spend time learning the facets of the disease or illness and empower yourself to make changes in your life or advocate for care.

There have been times in the VA when I could sense the counselor was perplexed by why I was doing so much work on my symptoms, and that was simply due to the fact I couldn't stop thinking "do they really understand me?" And from experience, some have, but many have not.

If you went to a doctor with a runny nose and cough and they responded, "take this and you will be fine." You then ask them, "is it a cold, the flu or an allergy," and they respond, "it's just a runny nose and cough." You would be perplexed as there are a number of other things you could do to lessen the symptoms. This is why you must know your symptoms and intimately. Some symptoms are the same for different conditions.

The knowledge you develop will not only help you understand

the vocabulary to communicate so you are on a more even level, but it will ultimately let you better understand the facets of the care you are receiving. And this is far more important, because in a bureaucracy, it can be slow and, unfortunately, the "squeaky wheel" approach sometimes has to be employed. You are one of many patients, and you must presume that the majority of work the counselor does for you is only when you are with them. I can't count the number of times a counselor did not even review my notes in the VA system. How did I know this? When I mentioned a topic of the past, I watched their eyes shift down to their computer screen.

My experiences showed me that the knowledge base within the mental health profession often comes across as too theoretical and not concrete or precise, like other topics in our lives. This is important because the inherent definition of a theory is that it is just that, and not absolute. It may also obligate you to ask "what" or "why" quite often so you can relate. To this point, take any mental health issue and do an internet search of a current topic or symptom. You may find they are all over the place in their theories and ideas and written in a near foreign language most can't comprehend. I like to think I am a pretty smart person due to my college education and profession, which taught me how to learn new and difficult concepts, and I found much of it to be undecipherable. It is my belief this is because the content is heavily weighted due to the clinical and academic underpinnings of their profession. There is of course a balance between the academia and the layman's world, but I feel the balance isn't as good as in the medical profession.

This, of course, creates a situation where you don't seem to be connecting with the provider or to the details of the conversation. It may also project they are book smart, but don't necessarily relate to you. I sometimes found to be subtle and sometimes overt, where I was thinking, "do they really understand me?" And why this is important is because you need to connect with your counselor so you can build rapport and actually accomplish something. If you have been in therapy, you intimately understand when you are just talking and not doing work, or you are being asked mundane questions, possibly from a rehearsed list. That is an element of therapy, but you will catch on when it isn't adequate.

In selecting a counselor, one concept that can be used is the 80/20 rule. We used this in business and it suggests 20% of the people do 80% of the work. Though in hindsight I think it is more like 90/10. Like any occupation, we all know a good proportion of those around us might be good people, but their work performance or work ethic may not be the highest. The mental health profession is no different, and I have personally found it prevalent in the VA system. While there are good employees, it is still a government bureaucracy of an epic proportion. This is not saying the VA is terrible, but I am saying that you will need to set your expectations to a reasonable level. This again is going to require you to learn to manage the content in your sessions and then advocate for yourself.

You might ask how you can tell if the provider is good or knowledgeable. To start, if they have a certification or degree, they at least demonstrate that they could memorize the material and pass a test. However, just because you can pass a test doesn't make you a good doctor or any profession at that. The signs are often subtle and admittedly subjective, but I think they are very good indicators. Another area to look into is their background on Linkedin, which may show you the number of years in the field, the longevity at certain jobs or practices, which you can also research online, and their tenure at their current position. This is not an absolute, but if you are veteran, it is good understanding of how much time they have spent with veterans. And, of course, do not hesitate asking the counselor about their experience as sometimes titles don't always match their experience as much as they do pay grades within the system. Meaning, what does a Senior title mean versus a similar employee who gets to use the title "Director."

Sometimes titles are just that, similar to what you see in non-profit organizations.

The first metric to measure the effectiveness of a counselor is the way and manner they ask questions. I personally have found the best counselors ask thought-provoking questions that stop you and cause you to deeply reflect. This, of course, is why you are going to a provider, to draw information out of you, often which is deeply buried or obscured by layers of other thoughts and experiences. I have had a couple counselors that mastered this, and they projected that they really understood me deep down. Conversely, I have had counselors ask questions that left me thinking, "is that the best you can ask?" Innately, you can pick up on this. Simply think of someone you've heard speak on any topic you may not know much about and when they are done talking, you think, "wow, they really know what they are talking about." Then there are people who project they are weak on a topic.

The second metric is passion. This is easier to key in on, particularly in the VA. As this is more obvious, I want to give you advice if the counselor is not passionate. After a few meetings you will quickly see whether they are going through the motions or using a list of prepared questions. If you feel your counselor does not have passion or you are not connecting, I suggest moving to another counselor. I personally have had a couple pretty poor counselors within or outside the VA. Early in my recovery, I remember going home and talking to my wife about my concerns. In hindsight, with a number of years of recovery under my belt, I discovered my intuitions were quite accurate. This, of course, is one of the benefits of having a heightened fight or flight engrained into your thinking. But I do caution you to be rational as some of the experiences could be your doing.

Another measurement is the longevity of the counselor within their profession, their specialty and the VA system. Just because a counselor has been in any of these areas for a period of time, it does not mean they necessarily understand the specific trauma you experienced. Like us, they can change careers. Most notably I have met counselors who feigned they understood PTSD. Through questioning them, I learned they did not intimately understand it in context to a veteran. More specifically, the first two counselors I saw prior to the VA never even diagnosed me with PTSD. It wasn't until I was in the VA that I met the first counselor who could intimately talk about the finite issues of being a Veteran with PTSD. They remained my counselor until I moved, and I still miss our interactions. But it does beg the question, how did the first two counselors not know how to identify it? Of course, that can't be answered, but those things I talked about previously gave me the indication.

Another thing that has often surprised me within the VA is that counselors did not know the five tiers of PTSD, specifically 10%, 30%, 50%, 70% and 100% that are outlined by the VA. The symptoms of these are different and hence why the VA pays you differently for them. If the counselor does not intimately know them from your questioning, they may not be a good fit. If you are not a veteran, I suggest reviewing these because the categories might help temper your broader understanding. It also can give you vocabulary and concepts to discuss with your counselor.

So how do you select a counselor? You will typically be offered whether you want a male or female counselor. If you are a veteran, I would suggest you ask if you can have one with former military service. Or, if you are a woman, you may choose to select a female counselor. This criterion may annoy some counselors, as they think they are fully suited for you. Possibly they are qualified, but if you talk with any veteran, they all understand how veterans communicate and relate to one another, no matter their age or branch of service. There is usually a quick rapport, but also an intimate understanding of what it was like to be in the service. This approach is true with other types of traumas as well. I have found the saying I heard long ago, "just because you stand in a garage, it doesn't make you a mechanic," applies to this. Just because one studies PTSD, or has talked to Veterans, does not mean one intimately understands it. As an example, would a person who has never been an alcoholic run an AA meeting? How is this different? It isn't. To this, ask for a counselor who mirrors your specific trauma. I can tell you from experience that this has markedly changed my progress. Now as a caveat, there are some counselors who did not serve that have "years" of veteran experience behind them, but again, this will project to you readily.

The last topic, which is more common now, is the use of online or telehealth sessions. The one benefit of this may be the fact you can get more frequent appointments as you are focused on time and not proximity. However, I would caution this does not replace human interaction where you are away from your comfort zone and the counselor can observe your body reactions. This also works for you as well to see how they are reacting or how organized their office may be. There should be a degree of balance with this.

One thing I do want to add here is that I mention I've had a number of counselors, and it may lead you to ask why so many? A couple I let go for obvious reasons, but I also moved to a different state and as well faced much turnover, which particularly happened during Covid and post Covid periods. In speaking with friends, some have had this issue and others haven't. This somewhat validates your need to know the counselor's longevity so you can foresee if they are going to last. Two times I personally experienced having my counselors turn over three times in a year. Yes, that is six counselors. While it was situational in part, it still got old and, admittedly, my patience was taxed. Try to anticipate this. The VA also uses college graduate level students (aka PhD interns) and you need to determine if that is adequate for you or not.

The second place to learn is a support group, possibly a PTSD-specific one, if available. I was fortunate to discover a Veteran PTSD support group in a city near me. This is possibly where I have learned the most practical information. The meeting chairs were former military and had combat roles, so the rapport was readily established. If you are woman and went through a specific trauma, there are often groups focused on that. But the fact that you are in a meeting with colleagues who are in different stages of their journey is significantly helpful. This is really no different than an AA meeting. You have people who have been sober for years and others who just started. And there is much to learn from both. The people with longevity in their recovery not only have wisdom, but also experience conquering the struggles of issues you are facing. Likewise, it is not uncommon that a younger person has a different, possibly contemporary, view of the world. The fact is you can learn from both, and more importantly, you can share what you have learned with them.

The third place to learn is from what I would refer to as passive resources, whether it be a book, hard copy or audio, internet articles, podcasts, social media and YouTube. The written sources go without saying, but I will tell you much of the detail can be too analytical, and there are a vast number of books on the topics. When writing this book, or memoir really, I never wanted to venture into that type of information. I could never write about the deep theoretical aspects of the illness and symptoms, but I was an expert on my own life and experiences. While I discussed this in the chapter HELPING, I found one of the best resources was YouTube, and I literally stumbled into this. I had used YouTube for years for various DIY or hobby interests, but I never realized the amount of mental health content available.

What I found on YouTube mirrored the metrics I mentioned previously to gauge a counselor. When you put a topic into YouTube, you will be surprised by the quality of the content to include the thought-provoking topics and passion these counselors have. What you will also find is that a number of counselors are recovering from issues themselves, which not only establishes a level of rapport but more concise guidance that comes from the heart.

I want to put a disclaimer here that YouTube does not replace a counselor, though admittedly, I have found at times that it has had better counselors than some I have had. Its real value is that it gives a list of topics, as well as the right vocabulary, that you can discuss with your counselor. What you will find is the words, phrases and context are things you can talk to verbatim. I can't tell you how many times I thought, "why hasn't this ever been discussed with me?" I would also caution, sometimes the content is not good and you have to use your judgement of such.

I personally use YouTube in a number of ways. Again, the value of it is the quality of content, and I can't count the number of things I learned from there that I had never heard discussed in my VA sessions. I remember one topic that I subsequently brought up and personally believe I caught my counselor off guard as I was able to talk about it. I don't know if the counselor actually liked that or not, but the fact is, it got me going on a thread that would help me significantly.

Why is this resource useful? I think there are a number of things that are in play. Firstly, most of these counselors are probably commercialized, meaning they get paid based on the number of people that watch them. To optimize this, which any YouTube content provider does, they ask you to subscribe to their page, so you will come back again. If the content is weak, you won't subscribe. I find topics quite concise, articulate and practiced, much like any presentation, but better since they are being recorded. The content of one video typically builds off the content in another video. This provides context and progress over time. Personally, I like the fact that these videos quickly discuss the topic (or issue) and get straight to the point. Videos typically range from 10 to 20 minutes, which is much shorter, but often more time-efficient than a counseling session. Admittedly, patience is not always one of my strengths, but then again, I have never liked meetings or sessions that plod along without structure and progress. That is just me.

Another aspect I find in many of these videos is that they give a list of tips how to acknowledge your behaviors and subsequently tips to changing your frame of mind, the processing of information and modifying those behaviors. I really like this approach personally and have this relationship from my counselor who helps me walk through a topic. In some ways, they mirror a life coach, who guides you along when you are stuck.

Another value is that being a video, you can watch it any time of day as well as stop it and repeat, which helps solidify the message. I really like this aspect and why I almost always take notes to discuss with my counselor. It is like setting up a meeting agenda so you are succinctly prepared. Again, I've really never liked going to a meeting that doesn't have an agenda or a goal, but this is sometimes the nature of counseling sessions. When you do take notes, mark the day you watched it and the source of the video so you can go back to it later. I also take notes from my counseling sessions and doctor appointments in the same book. This will let you go back and think further on a given topic. I go into this further in the chapter FORGETTING.

Now there is one final benefit of watching these videos and that it is how YouTube will post similar videos and content. I typically watch at least one per week for the reinforcement of concepts and have noticed YouTube subsequently posts some great content in my feed. If you are struggling with a concept, I think it is useful to hear different approaches and thoughts. Surprisingly, I have typically found that the content blends together and doesn't contradict one video to another. This most certainly is a function of the presenter's personal and professional experiences.

Remember, you are ultimately responsible for your mental health and the more work you put into it, the better grasp you will have of your well-being and better management of your progress.

And this comes back to mindshare. You are going to need to find sources, whether a counselor or content, that increase the positive information in your head. The more positive content you add, the more likely it will push out the negative content. Nobody will do this for you. Also, remember the counselor works for you. If they aren't doing the job that you expect them to or you aren't connecting with them, make a change.

THOUGHTS:

OVERWHELMING

THOUGHTS ON BRINGING PEACE TO YOUR MIND

Without question, one of the more frequent comments I hear from those with PTSD is the extent to which they feel overwhelmed and the difficulties they have explaining and managing it. But personally, I do not like the word "overwhelmed," much like I don't like the words "depressed" or "coping skills." All of these words, while usually well-intentioned, do not adequately describe what is really going on or what needs to be done. It's like saying, "I feel sick." These are in fact generic words created by the profession to easily summarize a bundle of sub-topics. I refer to them as "umbrella words."

I would however describe my most challenged periods with the expression "swimming in symptoms," which is an alternate version of being "swamped." Both of these terms are visual words and describe what is a "fluid" situation that ebbs and flows like waves, and likewise has the same power. Both of these describe a range which you might be feeling, somewhat like standing in a mid-size wave and floating through it or literally having a large wave crash down upon you. In my worst situation, it was like a massive wave crashed upon me, and my brain was like the frothy sand being spun around by the power of the water. So "swamped" seems more appropriate as you are struggling to recover from the massiveness of the situation.

The purpose of this chapter is to share the strategies of my waking hours or in visual terms, diving into the wave so its power won't completely consume you. I separate this from resting hours, particularly sleep, which I cover in the chapter RESTING. I do this because there are different approaches for them and that despite your best efforts, as daily life kicks in and more challenges arise, what you feel in your head is much like the constant crashing of waves. It just repeatedly continues and can feel unrelenting. At times, the things that trigger you, or even create anxiety or panic attacks, can shut you down. And in the middle of the day, this can create a difficult situation to navigate.

Not knowing where you are in your journey, you may be feeling things with a complexity and intensity that you have never felt before. It may feel quite strange, heavy, and powerful. So with that in mind, I want to explain what I felt and which you may feel in part. I feel this is important, because you are going to need help, which I discuss in the chapter HELPING. But the reality is that you are going to need to rely on yourself much of the time, as any help you get will be limited and possibly not as frequent as you would like or require. While I can't perfectly describe every scenario, I typically experienced the same group of feelings including being sad, scared, confused, betrayed and lonely. There are others to a lesser degree. The list is extensive, but typically these are simultaneous and the individual strength of these can vary from day to day and even hour to hour.

The fact is, one pool of feelings may be the same or different than another, and this is the challenge of using the simple word "overwhelmed," as each of these require different approaches. I would also argue, the better you can articulate what you are feeling, the better professional support you will get, as well as the empathy you might get from friends or family. I can certainly say the latter may not fully know what to do with you, and it might elicit the wrong response with insensitive or meaningless advice. The challenge we face having PTSD is these feelings are often extreme, and sometimes simple things can trigger a disproportionate response. The impact of these feelings can be utterly incapacitating. But having dealt with all extremes, I found a simple method to temper the chaos and bring some organization to what was going on in my head.

The first and foremost thing you need to address is whether you are safe. And I mean both physically and mentally safe. If you are having any suicidal ideation, contact the Suicide and Crisis Lifeline by dialing 988 on your phone. This well-established resource is excellent and has the capabilities to assist you with your feelings and thoughts. As well, if you don't have a counselor yet, you should also contact your Primary Care Physician and insurance provider so they can help facilitate the assistance you need. You should also use these contacts to fully disclose other aspects of your safety so you can get proper guidance. The rest of this chapter, however, is about developing a strategy to address the complexity of what is going on with your daily life.

That said, there is one thing I wish I understood early in my healing and that is your brain may be playing tricks on you. At my worst, my head was filled with a range of feelings and thoughts, and it often had me nearly mentally paralyzed. Looking back at these periods of instability, some of what I was thinking and feeling was logical and some of it wasn't. There is no doubt that some of it was being created in my mind from the extreme duress that I was facing. In order to move forward, you are literally going to have to organize your thoughts and feelings so you can begin dealing with them accordingly. More so, you can only deal with so many things at one time, so getting a plan is really important.

I was not familiar with the Serenity Prayer until a friend who was in AA shared it with me. The prayer, which was written by Reinhold Niebuhr, is actually longer, but it is the first part of it that many know. It goes, "God, grant me the serenity to accept the things I cannot change, the courage to change the things I can, and the wisdom to know the difference." This really got me thinking, as it covers the concept of "control," but it doesn't come out and say to understand the difference between things that are real and those that are not. And that is the crux of your strategy to gain some control of the chaos. I coined a phrase that I would say to myself regularly and still use it to this day. I say to myself, "is this real or is this not real, and can I control it or can I not control it?" This may seem awkward to do at first, but if you keep saying this, it will really help filter out some of the noise consuming you. Of course, things are not always fully obvious, but it gets you thinking in the right way to direct the feeling or thought into one of these groups so you can eventually deal with it.

When I broke down, I was living in a new city and had no friends. This was further compounded by the fact that my closest friends were hours away. I was literally stranded and attempted to make the best decisions possible, though in hindsight I wish I had made the decision to move. I was at a complete loss as to what to do and how to get some control over the extreme mental chaos I was experiencing. At the time, I had never been a writer, but for some reason I just started journaling what was going on in an effort to rationalize my messy and painful thoughts. When I've read some of this in recent years, some of it is logical and some of it is rambling. It is quite telling, though, in a number of ways, particularly how distraught and confused I was. There was one pattern, and it was continually asking myself complex questions, namely beginning with "why."

Years later I would come to learn that writing is very therapeutic and wish at the time I had received some advice as to how to explore this further. As I mentioned, you may not get as much counseling as you need or desire, but writing is possibly one of the most useful tools you can embrace quickly to help organize your thoughts. While you can choose to write anything you want, I encourage you to focus your writing with a purpose. This is the guidance I wish I had received. I did this to some degree, but it wasn't purposeful, though what I did do lent itself to developing concepts for this book.

If you are like I was, you probably have at least a dozen solid topics floating in your mind. Over time as my symptoms gained clarity, new topics came to play as others faded. To focus your feelings and thoughts to writing, the starting point to coordinating to smaller pieces is based on "nice versus need." If you have many issues like I did, you cannot reasonably address them all at the same time.

One approach can be writing about specific topics based on nice to do verses need to do. While all of what you are thinking may be important, some items are going to be crucial. Only you will be able to determine that, but issues such as family responsibilities (aka children), health, safety, etc. probably need to be addressed first. This is not easy particularly as life continues to march forward. Your writing does not need to be complete paragraphs and can contain comments, lists, tasks, goals, single words, etc. No matter what it is, I found one practice very useful long term and that was to underline a couple key words and add the date. Over time you may see patterns or it may help draw out other memories and thoughts.

Another approach to writing may be a way to simply tell your story, the history of your life. I found myself writing to myself looking for answers, though despite writing many things over and over hoping to discover the underlying meaning, it didn't always reveal answers I was desperately searching for. But this did not stop me. I also found myself writing to others, explaining what their decisions and actions had done to me. Because I realized at the time there would be little to no accountability or reconciliation, I never sent them. What did happen however is that I ended up writing to myself in the future. Sometimes that was the near future, if I wanted to rethink a certain topic or further out, when I wanted to review them with my counselor. And this is why some of it was logical and some wasn't. What I discovered is that I gained much clarity to my thoughts, and this ultimately allowed me to make key decisions to protect myself and my future. I discuss this at length in the chapter CUTTING.

Early in my healing, my vocabulary of my symptoms was not necessarily weak, but rather I can say it was probably not accurate enough to gain traction as fast as I could have. While you may have some experience with your types of symptoms, do not be surprised if you uncover different symptoms and terms. Unlike other health matters, I have found at times that the people experiencing the symptoms don't use the same vocabulary that those treating them do. And again, that is why I personally try to steer away from generic "umbrella" terms. Despite having a technical background, I vividly recall how hard it was for me to understand and articulate what I was feeling. In hindsight, a more methodical method of writing would have benefited me and also those I needed help from. As I note in the chapter FALLING, this was further compounded by the fact my feelings and symptoms were varying in intensity from day to day and sometimes hour to hour. Trying to put words to this can be very challenging, particularly if you do not have a full vocabulary to explain or express them.

One approach to understanding an array of complex feelings is to use the analogy of mixing paint colors. Except for black and white, all colors come from three primary colors: red, yellow, and blue. When these primary colors are mixed in equal parts with each other, you create the secondary colors of green, orange, and purple. But your feelings are not this simple, which is why they are so hard to explain. Specifically, one day you might be two parts red and one part blue and the next day it could be inverted. Even though both use three parts, the result is two very unique colors. And that is why in self-help writing, it is so important to think about your feelings in a different way. As an example, day one you might be very sad, very tired and a little angry; yet the next day you might have rested some and can be a little sad, but also very angry. Both days you can be feeling terrible, but the way you manage day one and day two may not be the same. In my case, though this may be an exaggeration of what actually happened, I never felt any day was the same. I felt as though I was constantly struggling to explain how I was feeling, and that is because the various degrees that you are experiencing with each feeling are changing. So as you write what you are feeling each day, attempt to identify your most common feelings and their intensity. Also try to note what may be going on and stimulating them. Even in recent years as issues have arisen, I have gone so far to do this twice a day to identify any patterns.

The next issue I often hear is how does one get control of these complex feelings that are swirling around. While trying to understand what is driving your feelings is very important, it may seem difficult to think or accomplish much with the way you are thinking. I know in my worst times, my thoughts were so complex and overbearing, I just wanted them to stop. This is where the Serenity Prayer is useful, where it says "accept" the things you cannot change. It is common for people to want quick answers. Meaning if you do these few things it will get better. This may be possible, but I don't believe I ever discovered what they are. You might be ignoring or distracting yourself from them or you may simply be in denial. As I noted before, some of these thoughts may or may not be real, so as the prayer also notes, you may need "courage" to go after them.

What I did discover is that when I slowed myself down, both my responses and actions, it helped lessen the severity of both the intensity and complexity of my feelings. Think of this like driving a car too hard when you are in a rush. You find yourself accelerating too fast when leaving a stop light. You then drive too fast, possibly over the speed limit, and then stop too quickly. If you do this, it creates a level of increasing anxiety and it takes a toll on the car. So just as you correct your driving to be more reasonable, this is what your goal needs to be with your racing mind.

The first step which I have trained myself to take, though admittedly I haven't always been successful, is controlling how fast and hard I react to something. Yes, there are times you have the right to be upset or in some cases you may be triggered by something that transpires. However, that is only the first part of that experience and how you manage it is the rest of the experience. In my case, I think my military training created a mindset of "mission," so my responses were tempered by a quick response to achieve a result or conversely to keep something from happening. While there is an element of this in our normal lives, the nature of our varied relationships is such that you just can't always blurt out what you are thinking, whether the situation is warranted or not. This, of course, takes practice, particularly when your primary thoughts may be derogatory. What you come to learn is that some of this is just a part of daily life. You cannot control those around you, or at least very much, and often you can't control what happens to you.

One place where I found my reactions being challenged the most was at work. Being in the corporate environment, I always felt the decorum and behavior of people should be inherently higher. This wasn't always the case, and I would periodically find myself more than annoyed, particularly when it came to customers. Being obliged to earn a living, I had to deal with them. In preparation, I would write four letters, "SDSU," on the top of the page I was going to take notes on. This would remind me to "slow down, shut up," and I would come to embrace this as a standard practice. It would also oblige me to listen more in lieu of talking or responding.

You will see that your anxiety will lessen as you practice this, and this in turn helps reduce this overall feeling.

The second strategy I learned was to embrace breathing in a more purposeful manner. I discuss this in the chapter RESTING, but I greatly improved the mindfulness of my breathing in three scenarios. The first scenario, which you may already be doing, is often culturally expressed as, "take a deep breath." This has a couple of meanings in context to the situation, but I literally mean it. I do this as I enter most situations, both friendly and hostile per se, and it is amazing what an impact this has on how you enter into that situation. Again, think of this like a car leaving an intersection. Are you going to "burn rubber," or are you going to rationally leave the intersection. The second breathing scenario is that during the majority of my awake hours, I not only slow down my reactivity, but I slow down my breathing. The driving a car scenario again works well here. Think of how you are cognizant of your speed while driving through a residential neighborhood. We do this for a number of reasons, but this is what you need to do with your reactivity and breathing. Be conscious not to go too fast and slow things down to the speed limit or less. This took me quite some time to master, as I am a Type A personality and quite "driven" from a work perspective. I guess we can generally call that "intense." There are many YouTube videos on breathing. Some content is better than others, but most will suggest the starting point of learning how to breathe is to breathe through your nose. When I started into this, I noticed how much I was breathing through my mouth. What I discovered was that I gained more control of my anxiety and anxious situations. The third breathing scenario is during my downtime, which I discuss in the chapter RESTING. This discusses breathing with slowing your final thoughts of the day.

The last strategy you may hear about is "grounding," and again, this is an umbrella term for literally dozens of supposed techniques. The fact is, there are so many that you may get confused. From my personal experience, some worked, but many didn't and possibly there are so many because people find different things to distract them from the moment, whether it be dissociation or a panic or anxiety attack. They, of course, can be used for other situations as well. Finding the right one might take some work and I caution you to consider them carefully, particularly those on the internet, as many of the posts are "sponsored" in an effort to get you to buy something or services. In the chapter HELPING, I expound upon this, but your fastest and most thorough advice may come from social media forums, podcasts or support groups. These are often your peers and you should get enough thoughts to help guide you.

The fundamental purpose of these grounding techniques is to essentially distract you and refocus your thoughts on more positive things or simply to bring you into reality. The two items I mentioned, consciously breathing and moving slower, are my favorites, but there is a third. That is going outside and being observant of the temperature, smells, wind, sounds, etc. In speaking with many with PTSD, this is one of the more popular ones. This is also a part of the chapter WALKING.

By going outside, many positive senses can be stimulated. This approach can often help counterbalance the negative stimulation or triggers that might have been created inside. The significant change in environment is what distracts your mind. Generally, being outside is a safe environment and does not typically overstimulate you, except for extreme weather. Admittedly, very hot weather bothered me for some time, but I had to mentally prepare myself for it. Overall though, there is something about the unique smell of plants and the feeling of the wind blowing across my skin that brings a calming sense to me, reducing my anxiety. And depending where you are, being outside lends itself to moving and breathing slower. What I find is the best strategy for grounding is to be present in the moment. Never lose sight of all the beautiful things around and be grateful for them, even the very small things. I taught myself to be prepared to use these approaches, but learned to embrace them subtly in my entire daily life. By doing this, I have found over a great period of time that the number of flashbacks, panic or anxiety attacks are lessened, as well as their intensity. Simply remember to think slow and be slow. The strategy you take to calming yourself won't be one thing, but a blending of multiple things that bring you comfort.

THOUGHTS:

RESTING

THOUGHTS ON RESTING YOUR MIND AND BODY

The topic of rest is probably at the top of the list of issues for all who have PTSD. Rest itself encompasses so many things to include sleep, relaxing, as well as resting both the body and the mind. The problem is however, this can be absolutely daunting as our body and mind may be out of synch with one another or just out of control. This becomes a much larger and complex issue, as your brain has changed. Your amygdala, where your fight, flight and freeze responses come from, may not shut off, making sleep challenging at best or, in some cases, an utter mess. We also develop habits or routines that are counterproductive to healthy rest and subsequently, we find it difficult to create a pause long enough so that we can rejuvenate.

My sleep patterns have been highly problematic for decades. It started very early in my military years. For those who have been deployed, you understand that this can be about the worst shift work a person can sustain. Our command had our division schedule at a relentless schedule, particularly when staffing was tight. One shift is the "4 and 8" rotation where you are on duty from midnight to 4 a.m. (aka 24:00 to 04:00 in military speak), after which if you are lucky, you might get one or two hours of sleep. You then go to your primary job until your next duty that goes from noon to 4 p.m. Technically, as you have relief duty and turnover, this extends your shift hours, further contracting your rest time. The following week you start your duty at 4 a.m. to 8 a.m. and it follows a similar pattern. This grinding routine could continue for many weeks and if deployed for several months. Coupled with drills, work, and sometimes general quarters, the amount of rest you got was incredibly small and fragmented.

For those who have ever worked off-hours shift work, you know intimately that this takes a toll on your body. The real danger to your health is if you experienced or are managing trauma during that period, you find yourself so mission-oriented that you do not really care for yourself. Personally, I remember the routine being so fatiguing that my sleep could be better categorized as passing out from exhaustion versus falling asleep. More so, in my workday, the only way to function or motivate my body to continue was to fill it with sugary or caffeinated drinks. I would embrace this behavior in the years to come.

There are probably few who haven't heard about the military or first responders who are well-attached to their coffee. If you look at this objectively, while it can be a necessary thing to do, it also damages your sleep cycle and health. If you have done shift work for years, you intimately understand this. The fact is your body was designed to sleep when it is dark and not to be driven by caffeine. While I drink coffee, I limit it to only the earliest part of the day as caffeine has a half-life that can mess up your sleep. I also completely stopped sugary drinks.

Interestingly, my nightmares and night terror did not start during my military service of six years or my college which extended four years after. It wasn't until my breakdown that it engaged and raged. I figure it was the culmination of all of my trauma that was more than enough to set it off. In part, I think that while college is much different than the military, in my case my habits and behaviors were quite similar. In high school my grades were only average to possibly slightly above for some classes, but I was never focused. The military taught me focus, and so while I was in college, I was still "on mission." As I was working on the difficult degree of economics, with a minor in statistics, my classes and studies, along with working part-time, kept me very busy. Again, I was sleeping due to exhaustion and less from just being naturally tired. I also recognize that this busy schedule for over ten years kept me so distracted that I ignored a very real problem.

After I broke down is also when the really big sleep problems started. I refer to this point as when my rubber band was stretched and did not go back to its original position. I discuss this, as well, in the chapter FEELING. At the time, I had PTSD but no knowledge of the concept. This might have hastened getting help, which would have included my sleep disorder, but I just wallowed in the pool of symptoms all hours of the day. For a number of years, my sleep could be categorized as passing out from exhaustion and then awakening to terror. This is the first point where my nightmares and night terror involved combat scenarios and also where I became physical. The reason I use both of these terms is that my rest was at varying intervals, times and intensities. Meaning, I would flail my arms, kick, scream, cry, sweat, etc. in different manners. And while you may not remember key details of night terror, you know it is transpiring when you end up sleeping in a strange position; your pillow is wet; your clothes or sheets are bound, and in my case, my hands were hurting. As I was flailing my arms, I hit my hands at times and had marks on them when I awoke. Other times I would pass out but only stay down until the nightmare woke me up. There were a lot of variants to this and for those who have been through it, you intimately understand the mental chaos.

Another thing that evolved is that I became afraid to fall asleep. Just like going back into theater or on an emergency response scenario, you know what lies ahead of you. At this point the damage had been done to my brain and I would embrace strategies and tactics to avoid going to bed. I once again found things I could be "on mission" that would go into the late evening. Usually, it was binge watching television or listening to music. It was avoidance, I knew I was doing it, but the lack of sleep and the exhausted body during the workday was far better than the terror of the night.

After I married, the situation improved over time, but I use the word "improved" quite loosely. Firstly, my wife who was a trained nurse was instrumental in helping me during the nights, and I can't even put to words how grateful I was. She would calm me down and put me back to sleep, often without me ever realizing it. For the first few years I continued having physical night terror, but it began to subside and by about 10 years in, it became less frequent. I cannot give any specific reasons or tactics I used, but I believe it was probably due to gaining more control in my normal life and over my symptoms. I also put up boundaries with people and things that triggered me. See the chapter CUTTING.

My overall sleep for about 20 years could be categorized as well below average. I typically never slept more than 5 to 6 hours per night, and it was not always connected. However, I learned to deal with it, though admittedly I was still tired and often burned out. I tried relentlessly over many years to find a solution, and nothing was working, to include speaking with scores of medical and psychiatric professionals. This was also being compounded by a heavy travel schedule, which not only kept me from my own bed, but sometimes had me in different time zones. And while different medicines were tried, most had little impact, and a couple actually made me sick. In that instance, I knew something was wrong, and despite explaining how I felt, I don't think anyone made the connection.

It wouldn't be until I met a seasoned psychiatrist within the VA who intimately understood my situation that I gained relief on a new medication that finally let me sleep a solid six hours, sometimes seven. There are, of course, still nights when I can't fall asleep and that can be due to many things. Sometimes I have caffeine too late in the day, had a light workday, or am just wide awake. But generally, since being placed on the right medication, I have maintained the same sleep schedule. The best advice I have is to be both patient and persistent with your medication and the doctor prescribing it. It does take time and hopefully not as long as it did for me.

Part of this is also positively influenced by the fact that I have a general sleep routine. In addition to avoiding certain types of stimulation, I developed a bedtime routine where I take my medications and go to bed at approximately the same time. This also includes not taking naps at all during the day, though I may make an exception if I am outright sick and need to rest. All of this together does not guarantee a perfect schedule, but if you do it, more often than not it will help to train your body to rest at the appropriate time of day. I realize some people simply struggle to sleep, even when they employ a number of these tactics. The only thing I found that marginally works is to get out of bed and go do some type of activity until I get sleepy. All of this requires patience and, in part, falls under the strategy "fake it to you make it." Meaning, you cannot give up on the routine.

The next level of rest is just that, rest, though it evaded me as well. Since being a child, I never recall not being emersed in all aspects of my daily life, particularly work. While being dedicated and focused on a job, it can overshadow the other parts of your life, specifically family. I believe I fell into the trap that if you work harder, you will do better. There is some truth to this, but it comes at the cost of many things I don't need to list here. Regarding PTSD, however, work can become a distraction to avoid resting and is an easy approach to rationalize doing it. For myself, I just could never rest. I felt as though I could never catch up to all of my responsibilities, and I just dug in and worked harder. This no doubt kept my mind elevated and let me ignore the subtleties signaling that my symptoms were worsening. I rationalized the hard work to life and also rationalized my symptoms to being tired and burned out. I was not fully confronting the fact I was not letting my body ever rest, which in turn would give clarity to many things I was experiencing.

One day I had an epiphany and thought of something I learned in one of my first physics classes in college, which is the Law of Inertia. While you may not know that law, you have most likely heard of Newton's First Law of Motion which says, "an object in motion stays in motion." This law generally says that an object in motion will stay in motion until something stops it. And for those with PTSD, that is exactly how our brains work. Our brain will keep going until something stops it, and this is possibly the best way to explain to others what is going on in our head. Our brain just does not stop thinking, no matter the time of day, and is why rest of any kind seems so hard to achieve.

It took me quite some time to learn how to rest, and admittedly, I failed trying a number of things. That is until I embraced certain habits and practices. As work was such a large component of this, that is where I will start. I recall when I first started working, laptops were still somewhat novel, and few employees had them. The value to this of course is that when you went home for the day, you left your work behind. As the cost of the laptops came down, more employees got them, and subsequently work followed you home for another hour or two. Then tablets and cell phones magnified this. This is where the first practice is used. Set a time that you will work each day and turn it off on that schedule. You may feel guilty, and some employers want you to, but your off time is your off time.

The second practice is quite close to first, and that is simply how and when you use technical devices. Without doubt, all of us probably spend too much time on our devices, typically viewing shows or social media. Understandably, you may be doing this to distract yourself, but as all of these emit light, it is continuing to stimulate your brain. There are different approaches to managing them, but mine was to use each device for its core purpose. I use my computer for the majority of my work and social media interactions, though at times I use it for streaming when shows are not on my purchased channels. I use my phone for making calls. What I found is that if I used my phone for all platforms of information, I was using it far more frequently and longer than I should. I was getting drawn into it for too much time since it is easy and convenient to use. And each time you hear a ding, you are essentially becoming Pavlov's dog. The repetitive and evasive "dinging" is keeping you from resting. To that, unless I am expecting an important call, and I mean important, I try not to bring any device into my bedroom. Like work, I turn it off at a set time for the day.

Finding things that bring you rest and comfort has been hit or miss for me. Having a generalized anxiety disorder has made it harder, requiring more preparation and diligence. Depending on how anxious a person you are, this will require you to evaluate many approaches. Some may work better than others. This anxiety level can be quite powerful and illogical. It can be the most beautiful day and I have no worries, yet my anxiety is raging. This is no doubt due in part to my ever-present hypervigilance. This consumes an incredible amount of energy and focus.

Two approaches that some have embraced are yoga and meditation. While they involve body and mind respectively, they both focus on calming oneself, with the goal of finding a degree of inner peace. This may bring you some comfort, but some with PTSD may find it does not. And that was the case for myself, though I attribute it to my having severe tinnitus. The ringing at times was so overwhelming that I found myself becoming agitated trying to ignore the ringing as my thoughts became calmer. I sometimes found music helped the meditation process, but not always, as the type of music or a specific sound or song could inadvertently pull me out of focus. I eventually developed a modified approach where I added calming music, typically instrumental, to a routine or downtime. I found this had the quickest results. It is a quick method to calm yourself and give a rhythmic pace that you can follow. This however requires you to turn the world off and just focus on yourself. This is awkward and uncomfortable at first, but it is achievable when making this a regular habit. This is also one use for which a cell phone is helpful if you stream music. It is important to learn how to slow down the pace of your daily routine.

Another approach to becoming more restful is to slow the pace of certain behaviors or activities in an effort to make them less taxing. For example, when I travelled for work, I typically found myself walking briskly, particularly when in the city. You can rationalize this as good exercise, but the driving force behind it can drive anxiety. When I retired, I made a number of changes in my "driven" mentality. The key one, and which many struggle with, is that you don't have to get up at a specific time and go to work. You are not in a rush to get dressed, drive to a client, open a computer or make phone calls. And that is where I made changes in my behaviors and habits. If you still work, evaluate how you proceed with the first steps of your day and create a slower, methodical process. Practice being more restful when you get out of bed and continue the pace for the remainder of the day.

The next thing I did was to prioritize what was really important to accomplish during the day or week. While you may have several things to do, limit the list, even if it means you only do the most important one. The very practice of determining "nice versus need" not only reduced my anxiety level, but dramatically reduced the forces driving me to do too much. I best manage this by keeping a single piece of paper that is segmented by the seven days of the week. Each day is comprised of three types of tasks including appointments, phone calls and specific activities. When the day is done, I use a checkmark to note it was completed or an "X" or "0" to note if it was cancelled or not completed. That permits you to acknowledge the status and that possibly you can finish it later in the week. We all do this inherently in our minds, but I found by putting this on paper, it took a great amount of detail out of my head. This subsequently reduced my angst about completing something and more so, almost eliminated the obsessing thoughts of forgetting something. While this may make you feel a little guilty, that is your brain telling you that and probably not the reality. Use your rest time to rest rather than thinking about the things you may or may not need to do.

Another thing I changed was how fast and intently I was doing tasks during the day. As noted, I have priorities each day, but I also temper the speed with which I complete them. And in a way, this is where the yoga and meditation concepts can be used. I discovered that if I slowed the pace of the task and how I thought about it, the less anxiety I had. And by "slowed," I mean a more methodical and repetitious pace. This slower approach may not only lend itself to a better result, but will help condition your body to be less reactive and tense. You will notice that the distance between your active and passive body states are much closer. Meaning the ability to put your body at rest is far easier, and it is not just happening because you are fatigued or exhausted.

The impact of reducing the number and pace of tasks was significant for me. The changes in my body were most noticeable by midday where I stopped hitting the famous "wall" after lunch. I attribute this to the fact I had not consumed too much energy too quickly, but I was also not being obliged to motivate myself mentally or with caffeine. As I mastered this behavior, I then applied it to all of my walking. I no longer felt obliged to walk fast and intently, but I walked at a reasonable pace and refused to be "rushed" unless necessary. A good example of this approach, which we have all done, is how we go to the supermarket. Did you use a list and did it include items for several days or a couple weeks? And when you went through the store, did you walk at a consistent pace or did you rush from item to item? It is, of course, okay to do this at times, but not all the time with every task. PTSD keeps our mind so busy and hypervigilant that to offset it, other parts of our lives are going to have to be slowed and paced. It was this very approach that started to positively impact the chaos in my head, and I began to slow and pace them. This is resting your brain.

An additional thing I learned was to be more conscious of my breathing. Again, this is part of both yoga and meditation, but I found that if I focus on breathing slower and through my nose, I felt my anxiety lessened. There is a good amount of research on this, and you can find detailed routines to practice. For me, it was simply to be cognizant of my breathing and being mindful to breathe slower and deeper. This practice does parallel slowing the pace you accomplish things during the day.

You may find certain hobbies or interests may bring rest to you, particularly calming activities. For myself, I find that outside activities—such as yardwork, walking or doing artwork—not only allow me to be creative, but allow me to manage my thoughts while doing them. No matter how busy you are, you can find 15 minutes or so to periodically do this. This could also include some form of exercise, though admittedly, that is not one of my favorite things to do!

The last concept, and possibly the most important, was to put my thoughts to rest. If your mind is hypervigilant or even obsessed with thoughts, it is good practice to put some of them to rest. To be clear, this is not denying or ignoring them; it is resting them. Some days I am just tired of certain thoughts and make myself put them to rest until the next day or so. If on the weekend, I will push the thoughts to Monday. You do not need to think about everything, every hour and every day. Heavy thoughts can be quite consuming and will drain your energy. More so, pervasive thoughts will keep you from resting. As you practice slowing your mind and body, it will become easier to find rest and put clarity to your PTSD symptoms.

THOUGHTS:

TRUSTING

THOUGHTS ON BUILDING RELATIONSHIPS

Without question, trust is the most important issue in the relationships I have had and continue to have. While there is much philosophical writing on this, it is an inherent value for those managing PTSD. It is a complex process that on the surface has many positive aspects, but it also comes with a number of negative ones I have found myself navigating for decades.

As I discussed in the chapter CUTTING, I became obliged to remove people from my life that I simply didn't trust, but more so did not feel safe around. These people have included family, old friends, co-workers and other casual acquaintances. But I have also put trust in the wrong things and in goals as well. Later, I would be obliged to prioritize what was truly important, and to some degree I must continue to remind myself now. I also had the most difficult person to trust and that was myself. Would the changes I was making in my life be right and could I trust myself to stick with them? The force that pulls you back to the past is strong and requires a different strategy if you want different results.

The first time I truly trusted anyone was when I joined the military. While you are learning many concepts from the first day, you hear trash can lids smashing in the middle of the night. The values of trust, integrity and honor were implemented quickly. It was the fundamental glue in the developing and joining a team together. It was connected at all levels and ranks. It was the paramount element that would eventually give you the confidence to know you were relatively safe. The person on your right and left had your back. You could trust they were looking out for you, and, conversely, they could trust you were looking out for them. All who serve in the military or as first responders realize this is a rare and precious relationship which is seldom repeated. But admittedly, I found this to eventually be an issue in parts of my military experience.

As my PTSD heightened, so did my trust radar, and in fact, it became fairly accurate. Your trust of people, places and things is directly tied to how you respond to things, whether it be fight, flight or freeze. You are highly attuned to always being alert and aware of threats, whether real or perceived. For me, I tend to both freeze then fight, but over time I have come to manage that. My ability to perceive threats, which typically fell into lies, manipulation, cheating, and gaslighting became quite good. And I don't believe that this was sixth sense, though at times it felt like it. I believe it came down to my initial military training. For those who did serve, you are quite aware how you are supposed to quickly respond and own up to errors or issues at hand. Fast forward into the present, if you were in the military long enough, gained rank, or moved into an occupation that required similar responses, it becomes fairly easy to identify how people should respond. This might include a combination of the tone of their voice, word choice, body language, and the confidence of how words are spoken.

Trust for me has become difficult at best. I have learned to accept that people are not perfect. At times I have felt as though I could trust very few people besides those with whom I've had a longstanding relationship. But having had a dysfunctional family, weak bosses, false friends and a couple unsuccessful relationships, I have unfortunately been afforded a broad range of scenarios that set the baseline for this. The hardest to accept are those that are close to you and thus you inherently have high expectations of. It's even harder when you have let someone into your inner sanctum of safety only to find they had ulterior motives or a selfish agenda. Betrayal, and particularly abandonment, can be quite brutal. You question if you can ever really get past it, in the sense you never really forget it. Admittedly, it took quite a bit of time for me even to be willing to make myself vulnerable at the most basic level and even more effort to actually try to trust new people. Even to this day, I seem to err on the side of caution with most everyone I meet.

One concept I want to discuss at this point is cognitive distortion. Is what you are seeing or feeling real or not? In fact, an issue for me has been that when I am under undo duress, I have perceived things inaccurately or more acutely. It will take practice to overcome this. Sometimes what you see is real, but other times it is not. And this comes down to control. Can you control this situation or not? I know I have made mistakes not because the people were necessarily bad, but they were not very competent in management or interpersonal skills. Things they said, which on the surface seemed off, were just due to the fact that they weren't good at expressing themselves. It is also possible that they, too, were dealing with some issue which caused them to act or respond similarly.

The first layer of trust that is the easiest to deal with is your work life. I have had a mix of employers with a couple having challenged management who had both compromised morals and behaviors. If you choose to stay with an employer, you will need to manage the relationship with boundaries. In the current market, there are far more employee rights, which probably has a lot more to do with the power of social media or the internet, rather than the companies actually caring about you. It is okay to say "no" and to use your chain of command or Human Resources. I know this is a difficult thing to do, particularly when you are financially dependent on a job, but it may come down to you preserving your mental health. I did leave two jobs in my career. I would categorize both as poor, and it was at many levels. It took a good bit of preparation and courage to leave. In hindsight, it was a very smart move and in both cases the level of anxiety in my life dropped significantly. You do not need to like or respect those you work with, but you have to get along with them so you can do your job. When you don't trust them or feel you are being emotionally manipulated, the decision to make a change becomes more urgent.

The selection of friends becomes trickier, as the set of values you measure them by are both different and much more stringent. However, in general it is very hard for me to make friends, and it has taken work on my part to learn how to meet and subsequently trust strangers. I most certainly was in the position of not trusting any new people. Looking at my friends today, most of my new friends were made in casual situations where we shared a common interest. That interest, in my case, was a hobby, and it gave me time to get to know them as we associated more over time.

Making new friends is no doubt influenced not only by my PTSD symptoms, as in being hypervigilant of my safety, but also that I have been betrayed by close friends. And by betrayed, I don't mean the person made a mistake, but mean they overtly did something that had a malevolent driving force behind it. Like family members, some long-time friends are quite close, if not closer due to the frequency of your interaction. One person comes to mind. We were quite close and shared multiple interests together. Their actions were so over-the-top it broke the fiber of our relationship. Not only had trust been broken, but their actions implanted the permanent question of what else had they done that I was not aware of or what else were they capable of doing in the future. The break was stressful, and I lamented over it for some time. This was further compounded by the fact they refused to apologize. Likewise, a couple relationships were lost over time simply because we evolved in different directions. This, however, is normal and can happen for a variety of reasons, whether it be value- or interest-based. Sometimes it is as simple as time and space that creates distance. Though I do have a couple of very close, long-term friends that I can pick up a phone and restart a conversation we had many months back.

In speaking with fellow veterans over many years, there does seem to be a general pattern that it is easier to make friends with other veterans. This no doubt comes from the many values that each of you share, no matter your branch of service. I can't count the number of times I have sat down with a fellow veteran, a person who was a complete stranger, and just started up a conversation with them and talked as if I had known them for years. I have done this with those in my hobby, but it is not as easy. Possibly this is the shared values are so different, like integrity, valor, honor, etc. While it is not impossible for non-veterans to understand these, it simply isn't to the same extent, though maybe with the exception of a first responder.

For me, PTSD has added multiple layers in the friend-making process. Having severe PTSD, I admittedly can be "touchy," as my symptoms are near constant. At times, it seems like work forcing yourself to talk and engage with people. More so, if they say something that annoys you, it seems easy to be polite and move on. This has required me to practice and to slow my thinking. As mentioned elsewhere in this book, I say to myself "is this real or is this not real?" I can absolutely tell you my mind plays tricks on me and drafts a narrative that is sometimes wrong. To be transparent, I have probably lost a couple of friends because of my behavior or words. This, of course, is looking in the rearview mirror knowing the person I am today is not the one I was. With greater understanding of how PTSD has and continues to impact my life, I am aware of what it was doing to me decades ago. It also means I have much different skills that navigate my behaviors and actions now.

The hardest relationship will be an intimate one. After my divorce, I absolutely loathed dating. This was not only due to a number of issues, but for the fact I was evolving into a different person. I had purposefully created a clean slate on so many aspects of my life, namely so I would not repeat my past mistakes. I wanted to create a new approach to life. In the chapter CUTTING, I note how I cut many things from my life, but in reality, I cut myself from my past life. But there is also the issue of fear. Fearing you will make a bad decision or even being rejected. All of this subsequently can lead to getting hurt and pulling you backwards. The one thing that worked in my favor is that there inherently became a good amount of time where I just focused on myself.

I recall when first dating, I was emotionally numb and that would continue for many years. To best describe my relationships at the time, they were more transactional, like a business transaction. When I met someone, I found myself measuring them, much like you are trying to understand the details of a business deal. My ability to emotionally connect was completely gone, and from notes I made at the time I just wasn't able to feel anything. At the time, I was quite aware I had been traumatized multiple times, but I was not yet aware of PTSD or its complexities.

At the time, I was incredibly lonely. There was never a time in my life that I wanted to be held more, but at the same time I didn't trust anyone to hold me. Again, my notes show I was absolutely lost as to how I was going to find an intimate partner that I could trust. Though I did attempt to date, I was falling very short of my expectations and have little doubt I was falling short of the other person's as well. This in part was the fact they weren't the right fit, but my belief looking back is my brain could not rationalize multiple feelings at the same time, or at all. My life was in survival mode, and while intimacy is part of that, it was being drowned by the numerous, negative symptoms consuming me.

To trust another person, you will need to make a number of

important choices. Some of these things may seem foreign and uncomfortable and they may require you to take risks. I cannot emphasize how difficult it was at the time for me trust a new partner. I recall that I didn't even see how it would be possible to trust again. Part of this was, of course, me just feeling immense pain, as in a broken heart, that was consuming every aspect of my daily life. But with my past and the array of people I had bad experiences with, I didn't see a path forward, as I simply didn't know whom I could trust anymore. An intimate relationship requires one to make oneself vulnerable, but I did not even know how or what to do. So many things had gone bad, and I was finally at my limit. I just simply couldn't go through it again and remained focused inward. This would continue for many years while I juggled shoring up the many broken parts of my life.

A number of years out I would meet my current wife. She was quite different than any woman I have ever dated. She too was a veteran, but she was also college-educated and street smart. Though she had a different degree, we shared multiple intellectual and personal interests. So a couple layers of the relationship were joined. The big difference versus other women I had dated was her values in context to her future life, meaning what things were important to her moving forward. She, too, had experienced challenges in her past, but she also shared the same dream of having a new future. At the time, I didn't realize the power of my selection process, but it came down to what I now call the Three F's.

The Three F's without doubt has been the most powerful tool I have used, not only in finding a life partner, but in measuring the strength of any relationship. The first "F" is faith. When I mention faith, this means different things to different people, and it doesn't necessarily infer that you go to church or not. In terms of a relationship, you want your faith to be balanced and similar. While it is possible, it may be difficult for a person who believes in God to partner with an atheist, or say a Christian to partner with a Muslim.

Your pool of faith beliefs and actions should be somewhat similar. Over multiple decades, my faith values have evolved, but fundamentally remain somewhat consistent. I also believe that meeting my wife just didn't happen.

The second "F" is family. At the time we met, I was still interacting with my family and hadn't fully come to grips with how their dysfunctionality had and continued to impact me. I was also concerned they, particularly my parents, would negatively influence relationships. In her case, her parents were exceptional people. Decades later I can still say both her mother and father were exceptional human beings at many levels. But the topic of family more importantly includes the future family you will share together. Our desire for a family was quite similar, and I can tell you that we both view our current family as one of the greatest personal accomplishments of our lives.

The third "F" is friends or those my wife surrounded herself with. At the time she was in the Army, so in general, she was surrounded with a good group of people. Also, having met her at church, I knew she wanted to be with the right type of people. There are other places you can meet good people, but you know the places that aren't good.

The Three F's are important in many ways. The most important is that it tells you where their head is at and what are their priorities. I did not want a person focused on worldly things, but things that are crucial for a more successful life. These three things not only become your support network for life, but they give you a metric of how you can better trust both their thought processes and decision making. A person who is materialistic may fear the loss of stuff over the loss of friendship. A person who is egotistical may put their wellbeing ahead of yours as a couple. A person who is hyperfocused on career goals may put their work ahead of you and a family. A person who is focused on faith, family and friends is more likely than not to share the mutual journey to building a future life.

Having been married nearly three decades, these values remain and have grown stronger. If I were to ask my wife right now what is most important, I can absolutely say it will be in one of these categories. And this is why my wife remains my best friend.

Getting over the trust hurdle is not easy. I still struggle with it at times. While I have given some of my approaches, your approach must be your approach. If you are in place where your life is in disarray or you are not feeling good about yourself, possibly waiting is the best. If your own self-image and worth is not high, it might well project to others. Look at this as an opportunity to work on a symptom that is adversely impacting your life. Look at this as an opportunity to create a new and better self. This in itself may have been the fundamental thing that moved me incrementally forward. I did not want to go back to the past and most certainly did not want to experience the fallout from broken trust to this degree again.

Like I was in my early recovery, I realize you might be in a dark place right now. I have never forgotten what that feels like and discuss this in the chapter FALLING. While trust is important, you need to put first things first. By this I mean, focus on the core feelings that are immobilizing your thoughts and keeping you from properly functioning. Trusting others is important, but if your health is off, you may not be able to trust yourself.

If you need to speak with someone on a more casual basis, your best option may be a counselor or support group. I speak about this in the chapter LEARNING, and this was one of the things that stopped some of the ongoing hemorrhaging of emotions. To be clear, it did not stop the issues driving the chaos in my head, but it stopped the dam from overflowing when I spoke to a peer who had been through the same or worse. At a minimum, it was giving me a chance to catch my breath with the wild thoughts running through my head, but more importantly, it gave me an opportunity to talk and be listened too. It provided an opportunity to have higher-level conversations involving emotions without any strings being attached. Having someone validate your agony is invaluable, but likewise, you may have experiences that help the person sitting across from you. And in that, you are establishing a level of trust.

When I have been asked how and when can I trust again, my answer has typically been, "when you are at peace with yourself." And by peace, I mean you are not at odds with yourself. You are ok with where you are heading mentally, though you may still be shoring up some of the weak areas of your life. Another part of this is you can't be in a relationship with two people at the same time. To be in a current relationship, you will need to be out of the old one and reduce the time spent on the old ones. I discuss this both in the CUTTING and FORGETTING chapters. If your decisions don't feel right, then most certainly talk with a counselor about them, or even bring the topic up at a support group. I assure you that this will get much response in a support group, because over time, trust is one of the key topics for those who have gone through trauma.

I'm going to end on the premise that trust is very difficult to rebuild, but it can be rebuilt. If you want a new experience, or more so a new life, you will need to be committed to making changes and possibly some very difficult ones. But the fact is you are going to need to trust some people at some point and even more importantly, you are going to need to trust yourself. Small and consistent steps will bring you forward.

THOUGHTS:

UNDERSTANDING

THOUGHTS ON COMPREHENDING YOUR MENTAL HEALTH

It is difficult to pinpoint when my healing process began, but I would mostly attribute it to the time when I mentally broke down. It's not that I actually began healing, but the past as I knew it had come to an end. If you have been in this position, you understand it is hard to measure how far you fall, but only over time do you see how far you have grown, and there are typically many steps to that.

My falling was in multiple plateaus, depending how I group the traumatic events. Though multiple life changes happened simultaneously and well after much of my trauma, it became the catalyst to the complex past. As my body and mind began to unravel, my trauma would pause and plateau per se, then fall to another lower level. Meaning, while I thought I had hit the bottom, more transpired and I sank to a much darker place mentally. In hindsight, the first drop was devastating, but the subsequent stages were apocalyptic in nature. Each step was literally instantaneous and completely consuming, affecting me both mentally and physically. I discuss these feelings in the chapter FALLING, but came to rest in a state where I was barely functioning.

Rightfully, anyone who hits the very bottom of their life wants something to grasp onto, whether good or bad, though some through denial may not acknowledge the latter. In my circumstance, I never really figured out what happened and through time, and a great deal at that, had to make assumptions. It is inherently human nature to want to know the W's, those including who, what, when, where and why. Possibly how is also desired, but that is a slightly deeper understanding of the intent that caused the trauma. For me, the key question I wanted to wrap my head around was why did these things happen. And despite asking why multiple times about specific points of my trauma, the answers were not revealing themselves. I not only wanted to understand why things happened to satiate my own questions, but more so to make changes so it would not happen again. I wanted to protect myself.

Depending on the type of trauma, some questions are profound and philosophical. If the trauma was caused by accident or intent, you might want to know why did God let this happen to you. If the trauma was inflicted by someone you know, you might want to understand why someone who should have cared for you did something so terrible. If you are a combat veteran or first responder, you might want to understand why you lived and someone with whom you were close to died or was killed. This may go as far as survivor's guilt. There are just scores of difficult questions you may be searching for and it can really consume your thoughts. The challenge you may face is that you could spend significant time looking for answers and those you find may not give you a complete picture of what happened.

But, of course, in the healing process, the lack of detail and information can make that process very difficult. The fact that I was dealing with multiple traumas simultaneously made it nearly impossible to discern what was causing what. I was unable to compartmentalize what was going on and just stop the chaos in my head.

So from the outset, I truly did not fully understand what had happened, what was happening or where I was headed. My mind was literally stuck repeating and repeating, which is referred to as rumination. And though I tried, I was unable to get answers about much of anything, and this further fueled the damage to my mental health. There was just so little detail and what I did think I understood was mostly illogical and fragmented. In hindsight, my understandings could have been wrong as well, but my overall reactions were not. And though it really wasn't different from the turmoil of my childhood or military service, being completely taken off guard so swiftly was the underlying issue. It's intensity after a very long period of relative calm magnified the situation. I couldn't put words to what was happening and that just derailed all of my thought processes. My mental health fully unwound, which subsequently triggered my physical health to fall with it. The details of all of my traumas were terrible on their own but combined put me in a place that is hard to describe with words.

So as I wanted to understand what had happened, so do each of us want desperately to understand the trauma that has derailed the various aspects of our life. We need the ability to rationalize the broad spectrum of feelings ranging from anger, sadness, guilt, hurt, etc. Even the most ardent denier, still inherently wants to know the facts, whether they admit this publicly or not. For myself, I was never in denial that it happened. The other situations and events happening at the same time made it quite clear. After many years passed, I still desired to have a basic understanding, though there really had been no revelations to date. I recognized my fallibility and felt it would help create a better path forward for myself. This never happened, and I was eventually obliged to make some basic assumptions, though they were fairly thin.

As you choose how you understand your trauma, there is a fine line between control and acceptance. Meaning, the control we use should be along the lines of life management and goal setting, as in the steps to your recovery and healing. And with acceptance, as you move forward, are you willing and able to accept what you discover about yourself in the past and more importantly, are you willing to use that information to help you move forward. I can't emphasize the word "control" enough because while we believe we have much control over the things in our life, it is often the case that we end up having very little. We also find ourselves trying to control the wrong things or try to control too much of the right things. This of course is our desire to protect ourselves from being hurt again. It is tied to our fight or flight responses engrained in most of our thoughts.

Yet as I began to heal and gained a very basic foothold of my mental health, though admittedly that was a fair amount of time, I was willing and able to make changes, even hard ones, to move my life forward. Fortunately, and possibly unknowingly, I made some of these changes early in the process. The things I made changes on, I had varying levels of control, but they were subtle. I eventually began to recognize those things I could or should control while letting other things pass.

So in my search for understanding, I did a number of things. The first thing I did was to research extensively the many factors in my traumas, both the causes and symptoms. This was not done to become an expert on those factors, as much as it was an attempt to understand what was happening to me both physically and mentally because of them. So being a novice in these matters, I went to libraries and bookstores to investigate self-help books and literary periodicals. And while I did find some snippets of what I was experiencing, it honestly was surprising what I didn't find. To me, it seemed as though the professionals or those who showed a general interest in the topics, could speak of the issues, but not about the issues. Much of the detail was rambling, technical jargon or winded, philosophical diatribes that lacked the emotional explanation and quantification of the chaos and damage. This of course is much like a non-veteran book writer who attempts to write about a combat story. While they can read another book or watch a movie about it, it is hard for them to write intimately about it because they have not experienced the horror. They cannot express what is really like to be in that degree of violence. Those who go through trauma want to understand why they feel absolutely terrible in so many ways and what they can do to make it stop.

The second thing I did was seek professional counseling. Over the years I visited a number of counselors, but like the literature, some of the meetings were futile and vague, and I recall leaving more drained than when I arrived. And in this one area, I remain very critical. It wouldn't be until I received focused PTSD counseling at the Veterans Administration (VA), that I found counselors who truly understood every aspect of the trauma I had endured. But to be clear, I also found problematic counselors at the VA as well.

This would only harden my position about early counselors that I felt had no clue of what I was talking about, or possibly they were just watching the clock. The sessions were often a methodical list of questions that were sterile or in some cases lacked any depth to help reveal the underpinnings of my issues. I often recall thinking whether the counselor even knew what they were doing. At other times I would be perplexed wondering why the questions were so weak. And when the time was up, the session turned off like an egg timer. Quite possibly the literature I read was written by academics for academics, and consequentially, explained why my numerous experiences with counselors were uneventful, if not useless.

Now to be fair to the counselors, maybe much of this in the past had to do with the general lack of understanding of PTSD and the cultural awareness and acceptance of it at that time. This is still an issue today, but the research that has transpired and the cultural softening towards people with mental health issues has expanded significantly. In hindsight and not having specific notes, I wondered how these counselors never pegged me with PTSD. What I recall them saying was "depressed," but in context to the contemporary understanding of PTSD and depression, it was a grossly inadequate assessment. Again, I talk about this in the chapter FALLING. I was not in a steady state called "depressed," but in a very fluid state undulating between a variety of symptoms. My mind was in full chaos.

As I have spoken to scores of groups and mentored others with or effected by PTSD, I really emphasize the importance of finding the right counselor. To be clear, I am not just talking about qualifications or whether you like the counselor, but are they helping you to stop the mental hemorrhaging or helping you grow in a meaningful direction. You will be able to determine this quickly if you are honest with yourself and after a couple meetings have the courage to cut loose and try another. Remember, you are not obliged to them. This is your life and time is of the essence. The longer you remain at the same level of anguish, the more likely there will be a multiplying effect on your well-being. Had I been able to find the right counselor earlier, I believe I would not have suffered to the degree that I did.

The third thing I did, and this was quite early on, is that I attended a divorce recovery group sponsored by a church. This step would be by far the greatest impact to my understanding of where I was in my life at that time, as well as an assessment of all of my personal relationships. Each person had their unique story. I was probably one of the youngest. But, the sessions were based on listening and sharing, but more so on the articulation of great life wisdom. So for the first time in my life, I was in a room of adults intimately sharing complex feelings and subsequently watching others show great empathy for one another.

Interestingly, this was the turning point of my faith. For the first time I saw the blending of love and religion together in a non-oppressive or bloviated form. I would go on to meet a handful of people who had a significant impact on my life and faith, and who I can directly connect to the person I have become. One person I met there, almost 20 years my senior, would eventually become my best man and godfather of my eldest son. He also became a father figure, something I really never had. Another, who led the group, would inspire this book. And to this day we remain close friends.

I would subsequently go to combat-related PTSD support groups and likewise found much of the same. The ability to connect with those with a similar mindset was crucial in me getting both validation and broader answers to life. This in particular helped me to come to grips with what can be peculiar, dystopian-like experiences. Some of the things I have experienced or have heard from fellow veterans can in itself be hard for a non-veteran to comprehend. There are just nuances to the environment or situation that are very difficult for people to fully understand. I believe first responders also go through a similar situation. Possibly, this is why some counselors are partly ineffective as they just don't get the full experience.

There were times that my expectations were probably too high. Many people are not prepared or willing to discuss or make the changes based upon what they learned. But coming from the edge of death I clearly came to terms with the fact I would not go back there. And I did not really understand how close I came to death until I began healing. I remember looking upon my healing and not only thinking about how far I came, but how sad and frightening the situation was. As I kept doing this many times in the following years, I kept coming to the same conclusion, seeing how far I had yet come again.

But with a couple of decades behind me, there are things I learned that may help you better understand and begin your personal recovery journey. First and foremost, despite you believing that you do deserve answers, the harsh fact is that you may never figure out what happened or fully understand it. This certainly happened with me. As my faith and my academic knowledge of PTSD and its symptoms became stronger, I would come to understand how strange life can be. Simply, life is quite unfair at times, but that is just life.

With these thoughts in mind, I want to shift back to the concept of control. Trying to find answers and understanding of your trauma is a level of control. While it may not be unreasonable to want answers, sometimes they just don't exist. But what if I were to position the concept thusly: does it really matter if you don't find out all of the truth? The fact is, good people can do bad things. Likewise, really bad things can happen to good people, whether by accident or on purpose. Life can simply create a string of events that are not even connected and intended, yet they can create a world of havoc. And there are simply scores of these scenarios that can upend your life and leave you completely bewildered and mentally crippled.

And it was this very concept of control that made an enormous impact on my life several years into healing. I came to the realization that I had far less control over a number of aspects in my life than I thought I did. I also came to the realization that the more I attempted to control aspects in my life, the less control I seemed to have. Likewise, the more control I relinquished, the more control there seemed to be. This gave me part of the understanding of the past I was looking for. The understanding that at times there is no understanding. Sometimes there are no answers to be had, but years out, possibly you will look favorably upon the fact you were fortunate not to learn certain things.

There is a downside as well to trying to understand some aspects of your trauma if you are under duress. Your thoughts may be so overwhelmed that you may not accurately assess the details, nor process them in the right way. This does not invalidate what you are thinking or believing, but it also may be better to write them down, giving you additional time to think about them. Meaning, time will often give you wisdom or insight to see with a certain level of clarity. It may also allow more details to surface and subsequently may let you bundle the thoughts together to address them in the most supportive way.

I have become better at this, but at times it still challenges me. I have to remind myself of the skills I have developed and put them to practice. What I have found that works best is trying to place the details into two categories: what do I really need verses what I think I need. There can be a thin line between these two, but it most certainly helps your thought processes. And without doubt, the more issues and detail you have floating around in your head the more anxiety you may experience. If it goes too far, the detail can just go in repeating cycles, holding your thoughts to the past and possibly clouding out progress. Get your thoughts out of your head and put them on paper. Ask yourself, what do I really need right now?

As I reflect back on the most challenging years, what I did not see were the positive changes happening to my life. While I had lost some people, I most certainly gained new people who more fully enriched my present. While I had gone through much trauma, I found this was the groundwork for me to accomplish many great things for veterans. Had I not had these experiences, I absolutely would not have been able to have the empathy and understanding to take a leadership role in substantial undertakings. In fact, I would come to understand that some of the most horrible things that had happened to me were a blessing. It obliged me to give up looking futilely for answers and understanding, but simply to place them as life experiences that had empowered me to do great things in the future.

If you are emotionally hemorrhaging, I encourage you to seek out a support group and counselor as this may be the quickest approach to bringing a degree of understanding to you. Many of the things I observed and learned helped me to understand that while my situation was bad, it was recoverable. It also allowed me to be on an emotional parity with others, giving me a sense that I was not in it alone.

Likewise, do not expect your families or friends to be of any significant assistance. While they may care for you, they can be biased and tell you either the wrong thing or not have the right answers. And to be fair to them, they may be tired of hearing from you. Many of my longer-term friends, particularly those that were married, didn't seem to know what to do with a single person or one who was suicidal. And I think naturally, those friendships slowly dissolved away as their interests and lives were moving in a different direction. A support group will provide an intimate environment that will give you a platform to understand yourself and a number of things influencing your life.

If you are also dealing with addiction, this should not replace the primary support group and should be with the respective organization. And though I am not an alcoholic or addict, I have been to many AA meetings and will tell you that in one of these small rooms I have heard some of the best messages in my life. Addiction, as you may know, is a nasty disease, and it is ever present. You may not fully understand why or how you became addicted, but you can most certainly learn skills to slow or prevent you from continuing to be one. This does complicate your overall recovery from PTSD, but I would argue it needs to be done in parallel. It may also give you a different clarity to your understanding of what happened and where you are headed.

In my personal relationships, I have found those in recovery to have some of the strongest spirits and wisdom. I would estimate somewhere between one third and a half of my closest friends have faced this dilemma in their life and believe they would concur in the advice I have given. Over the years, I can't define the amount of advice and wisdom I have received from them. Not only has it greatly helped me with my issues of the past and at hand, but it has tempered my understanding of all aspects of my life. It has also enforced my understanding that with work that I will continue to heal.

THOUGHTS:

WALKING

THOUGHTS ON PHYSICALLY AND MENTALLY MOVING FORWARD

It wasn't until I mentally broke down, that I was taken past a point I had never been to before. Despite all the trauma I had been through, this time my mind and body literally became numb. It's like when you slip on ice. In that very short period of time as gravity takes hold, you can feel your body falling; yet you cannot think quick enough how to break the fall. You know you are falling and there is basically nothing you can do as the pain and anguish quickly set it. But this time, however, both my mind and body collapsed from the overwhelming agony. When I literally fell to the floor, I had come to a point where I could not physically move. And I stayed there for many hours completely lost to reality as the mental fog set in. What had happened to me was bad. The totality of decades of trauma took hold. And while I believed at the time that I had hit bottom, my situation would get worse, and it would take many years to rejuvenate.

While this chapter is titled WALKING, it really is about moving, both physically and mentally. For those who have been traumatized, walking is a major achievement, particularly when basic movement to accomplish the most basic things seems to be unachievable. Both your mind and body seem at odds with each other and the will to do much of anything is distant. After I started my journey towards recovery, it took me a very long time to become active. I use the word "active" loosely as I am inferring many other things that are distant from exercise or purpose-driven walking. I am talking about getting out of bed, getting off the sofa, doing basic chores, going to work and, in my case, the desire of even wanting to go outside. Walking wasn't even a thought.

My most prevalent state of being, which I discuss in the chapter FEELING, was being numb. It didn't matter what I was doing or when, I was not only mentally numb, but I also was struggling to feel things physically. From the time I woke up until the time I went to bed I felt this way. It was particularly difficult when I was with others. I'm not sure if it projected to them, but knowing the "gaze" now, it must have shown to some degree. I knew my ability to actually feel and interact with my surroundings was nearly gone as I strongly embraced isolation. I had to make a living and was a good actor, but I limited my exposure to others by retreating to my apartment in off hours. I vividly recall that my face often felt similar to being out in very cold weather. I could push my finger into my forehead and while I could feel the pressure of my skin being pushed in, the actual feeling was tight with a very dull sensation. My body was like this as well and would remain in this state for a number of years. If I tried to push my body to move too much, it would ache as though I had been physically active, much like the feeling after you run. But this of course was completely opposite to the reality. To this day if I have a panic attack, my face feels the same and that is also where I typically hold my stress.

For the first few years after my breakdown, not only did I not want to do much of anything, I wanted to be left alone. By day I would go to work and do what I had to, but after work, I slipped back into my state of avoidance. I recall having generally good work reviews, yet I barely remember my work at that employer. I presume it was my "mission-oriented" mentality that let me push through it, but have no clue how I pulled it off. Without doubt, being numb did have a benefit, though, as it was a safe place, as it isolated me from feelings, both emotional and sensory. Small things would periodically derail me, particularly certain noises and smells, but in general, I could not feel them and just ignored them. I also didn't create any new close friends and that evolved from me losing the ability to trust people. This created a situation where I prevented interaction that might have helped me feel something, but the risk and subsequent fear of more mental anguish far outweighed the perceived benefits. See the chapter TRUSTING.

Even decades later, if I am given a choice to do something public or be alone, I will choose the latter. Though now the difference is in my alone time I am doing something creative or productive. And this is really how life is, as it keeps moving forward, no matter the condition you are in. Yes, the situation you are currently in might be difficult and unfair, but accepting that the path forward is not a clean or fair one, is where you have to set your mind. At some point you will need to get moving to either accomplish basic tasks or move on with your life. Walking is a good and safe compromise.

I don't recall how I became focused on walking, but it just happened. After the breakdown I was flat out exhausted all the time. In fact, for what would turn out to be years, I could not even rest or sleep, so my energy level remained quite low. This was also compounded by the fact I was severely isolating myself any time I was not at work. I would come home from work and just collapse and drift away gazing into the walls and mentally disappear. See the chapters ISOLATING and RESTING. My ability to get moving was also no doubt thwarted by the fact I really don't like to exercise in the traditional definition (aka cardio). This probably was created by the fact that after the mandatory PT and drilling in the military, I really came to disliking exercise. I would later joke "when I got out of the military, I vowed two things . . . one, I won't ever run in combat boots again and two, I won't ever run again." When I see people exercise for hours or run a long marathon, I am truly in awe. That was not and still is not for me. And while I now know walking is a part of exercise, I did not view it as such at the time.

For me, walking would become one of the key steps in my recovery, though I would say at first it was more a function of wandering. But in the simplest of terms, it did get me moving. And that was my problem. Except for work, which was mostly sitting at a desk, I neither really wanted to, nor could I move in any capacity. For the stranger to mental health issues—be it a family member, friend or co-worker—does not fully understand this inability to move or be active. At times, I wonder if some of my therapists truly got it, as well. Sadly, we often hear the insensitive "suck it up" or "get over it" from those closest to us, but this inability to move is very real. As I look back upon it with much experience now, it perplexes me how far I had fallen and the depth that my mind and body were frozen to inactivity. No matter how hard I attempted to motivate myself, for many reasons the "off" button couldn't be turned "on." I just wanted to be left alone and stay in a dormant-like state, though I did know to some degree that I had to do things. Work was generally safe and as much of my work was independent, it didn't require me to spend much time with colleagues. But, to put context to the depth of my mental state at the time, I didn't realize how very sick I was or that I was going through a mental breakdown.

Though I had experienced trauma a number of times before, the length of time to emerge from this period of my life was surprisingly long. What I was experiencing was complex, and I really struggled to put words to it. No doubt this was due to the fact I was not comprehending the totality of the details and how ill I was. The best way I would explain this to future therapists is that I felt like a rubber band that had been stretched one too many times and wasn't going back to the original state. I realized that I was suffering depression to some degree, but my actual situation was far more complex and I had broached the boundaries of a number of illnesses and disorders that took years to diagnose. That of course includes the diagnosis of PTSD. I'm not sure if anyone observed the severity of my situation besides my sister, but I probably should have been hospitalized. This, however, was not an option at the time as I had no local support, so I remained in this state for much longer than I might have otherwise. I believe had there been some level of intervention, my journey to healing would have been hastened. Like the overstretched rubber band, however, both my body and mind were not springing back into shape and it would take many years to noticeably improve. The chapters DRIFTING and FALLING discuss this more in depth.

I do not recall when or how I chose to become active. But wanting to move and being able to move are, of course, two very different things. While part of it is intent, the subtle issue is more than motivation, or depression, but that the outside world did not feel safe to me. And for a period of time, while I knew I should move, I also felt like I was unable to move. I went through a few stages with becoming active, but it is unclear how it fully evolved. Keep in mind, you are probably going through multiple issues and symptoms simultaneously. During one week your symptoms may be weighted in one direction, while the next, it changes. So as an example, one week my depression would be very high, while my anxiety and fatigue were at a moderate level. The next week these symptoms would flip. This regularly changing state of being not only kept me from being able to grasp the details of the moment, but created this fluid reality that was outweighing both good and productive thoughts. As you self-reflect, understanding that this change of state can happen and feel peculiar is important to your comprehension of the dynamics and complexities of your symptoms. And this is what weighed me down into inactivity and consumed what little energy I had to do even basic things. I simply couldn't think "forward," and, hence, I couldn't move forward.

At first, I would walk around my apartment complex, the downtown business district and a couple of parks that weren't far from it. I cannot pinpoint what finally got me out of my apartment, but believe it was probably boredom. We didn't have the internet, social media or video content that we do today, so music and reading were a bigger part of your off-hours. Like today, I know that I could have only taken so much of that, as I did not have any developed hobbies at that point. My apartment was in a hilly area so walking wasn't easy and, as well, there was traffic in most of these places. The city I was living in at the time had the remnants of a canal and the old tow path was converted to a trail. It was a Sunday afternoon when I decided to investigate it. I would come to really like this trail and would eventually walk it hundreds of times. While there were other people there, there typically weren't many and the towpath was wide and smooth. It was easy to walk with minimal effort. I presume at first I was shuffling my feet more than walking.

But, despite being outside, I remained in a state of isolation. Meaning, even though I was walking, I was still lost in my own head and not interacting with the world. I can still feel this way now, though it is managed and not nearly to the same degree, so I have a good understanding of how I was acting and reacting to my surroundings then. This of course comes from healing and my thoughts were very distant and probably like the mule that once pulled the boat down the canal, I was just walking and pulling my symptoms behind me. The subtleties of being outside were, however, reaching me. There would be momentary respites where I could smell or hear something that was appealing. Your life might feel like a complete mess, but one can always find something positive to latch onto, and for me, walking was one of them. The actions you take, whether it be walking or other, must make you feel safe. So, I kept returning to this place and continued to walk.

Moving is an issue for many people, and having met many over three decades, this is one of a few common comments. Moving has to be a goal. The troubles you may have can be complex and deeply rooted, and they may not go away for a while. But life in a sense can be cruel and keeps moving, sometimes with you and sometimes without. Your situation could be the same for a month or years. My state, being at the most severe and critical level, would last for a few years and would continue at a moderate level for at least another decade, though it would be two decades until I fell into the category of being disabled. Part of this was my doing, as in not giving up the fight, but also that new symptoms and the depth of them evolved over time.

It is hard to measure depression, though in the rearview mirror, which is 20/20 vision, and having an understanding of your health at the moment, you can calibrate, "I must have really been sick." Decades later, I am amazed how I endured what I did and where I was at both mentally and physically. It is shocking really, and were I to have a video of myself, I know I would say, "that's impossible, that can't be me." But it was.

If you don't want to get out of bed, or to be out in public, you are probably suffering the symptoms of depression. There was also the issue of just not liking people. We may joke about this at times, but I really did not like people. Or I just couldn't or wouldn't trust them. People who I should have been able to count on and trust, repeatedly failed me. Of course I own some of that, but when it starts as a kid, you don't. And looking back on myself as a child, that is where I began to isolate myself, though I coped in different ways. As a grown adult though, it was different. At the time, I also faced the reality that there really were no more people I could trust in a way I needed to, and it was going to be my journey. And I can say, much of my life to this day can be categorized as a solo walking journey.

Walking is a good compromise when done in the right place. It is also an excellent goal that can remain somewhat consistent when nothing else is. Did I have these thoughts early on? No, not even remotely was it in my thoughts. And though one might think to instinctively go for a walk, most of us seldom do it or at least not without prompting. Without doubt, this is one of the most incredible gifts we take for granted, yet one of the most powerful tools we have in recovery. While most of us do it all day long, it is probably the best activity that can take us away from our troubles. For those that are unable to walk, this applies to becoming mobile in a wheel chair or electric scooter. Obviously, your troubles may still be there when you are done, but the goal here is to get a break from them by doing something that is positive. Looking back at my later life over the past couple of decades, these small positive experiences are what I latched onto and what pulled me out of the isolated and negative state that I was in.

Walking also triggered a release from the chaotic world. While outside, the subtle stimulations, whether the temperature or wind, was enough that I could feel them whereas other stimulations, like noise, quickly overwhelmed me. Over time, there would be favorite places I'd like to walk, most of which were low-level trails that took minimal effort like river walks, public forests and large parks. To this day, the simple smell of the woods or cool breeze on my skin, takes me to a place of solitude. This is probably a combination of my current state of being, but I have also come to understand it was a tool that would pull me out of my negative state.

Years later I would come across an article on "forest bathing," which put a term to what I was experiencing. There are a number of variants to the definition, but for myself, this was a form of grounding. Having journaled extensively on my walking in the early years, I see a pattern in my entries where a small group of senses were being positively impacted. These typically ranged from smells, such as Fall leaves, or feelings on my skin, as though the wind was softly caressing it. In warmer weather, I would note the warm, saturating feeling of the sun on my skin or the unique smell of certain plants, like pine or flowers. To this day, those feelings and earthy smells quickly take me to my happiest place and is also why I thoroughly enjoy gardening and yard work. But the key element is that your experience be in a quiet place and by walking in a controlled manner, you can slowly move in and out of these at your own pace. You can experience these feelings in a safe way, so they slowly stimulate you without inundating your overall senses.

What I would come to discover is that these walks would begin the process of reprogramming my entire sensory system. And while I was finding great comfort in them, the impact at the time was far greater than I thought it was. It was a step towards moving forward from the vast array of negative feelings I had gone through for so many years. Yes, there were still some negative feelings, as in muscle aches, but in a cognitive way, they were only negative because that is normal. They weren't self-induced, such as a bad behavior or someone perpetuating them upon you. The totality of the experience was positive and the investment by me was safe and controlled. I had come to change my mindset that everything isn't bad.

Having walking goals is a good thing, as it is much better to have a short, successful walk than a longer one that isn't. Just getting off the sofa and walking to the corner might be a huge success. But having growth goals is also just as important, meaning next week you might choose to walk farther or somewhere specific. Another goal is to use this walking time purposefully for specific topics. In advance, I was committed to not thinking about certain things. This does not mean you will ignore them, but that you are focusing on select ones. Your mind may be cluttered with debris, but this walk is intended to give your mind a reprieve from it, even if only for a few minutes. This will take practice. In the early years, I was certainly obsessed about the details of what happened, but they weren't going to change, and they would never fully reveal themselves. If you go on a walk and dwell in the vast complexities of the past, your recovery path may be more challenging, no matter how far you walk. Small steps are often big steps. Small successes are often big successes.

I have often been asked, "how do you know when you are healing?" The answer I believe comes down to the one word "joy." Walking evolved to me really enjoying the positive senses being stimulated and the experiences being created. I had moved from a dark world and a place of not wanting to be active, to looking forward to walking. I vividly recall the world where I found no joy, as well as how long and difficult the journey was. Yet I have chosen to keep walking both mentally and physically. No matter how dark and endless the world may seem, it is important to keep walking forward. Yes, moving forward was difficult, but I persevered and realized over time that, as I was walking to and from the shadows, hope was creeping into my world. And while you may not feel like moving, it simply starts by putting one foot in front of the other, even if it is shuffling. Remember to look forward, work hard and keep walking as it is the light that creates those shadows. As you continue walking forward, you will continue to leave the darkness behind you.

THOUGHTS:

Printed in Dunstable, United Kingdom

79714343R00107